ALICE HAWKINS

AND THE SUFFRAGETTE MOVEMENT IN
EDWARDIAN LEICESTER

ALICE HAWKINS

AND THE SUFFRAGETTE MOVEMENT IN EDWARDIAN LEICESTER

Dr Richard Whitmore

Alice Hawkins

To my mum Vera and her cousins Madge and Joan for keeping alive the memories of their valiant grandmother, Alice.

First published in Great Britain in 2007 by
The Breedon Books Publishing Company Limited
Breedon House, 3 The Parker Centre, Derby, DE21 4SZ.

Paperback edition published in Great Britain in 2012 by
The Derby Books Publishing Company Limited,
3 The Parker Centre, Derby, DE21 4SZ.

ISBN 978-1-78091-127-4

Printed and bound by Copytech (UK) Limited, Peterborough.

CONTENTS

Acknowledgements 6

Foreword by Rt Hon Patricia Hewitt 7

Foreword by Peter Barratt – Alice's great-grandson 9

Introduction 10

Chapter One
Radical Traditions and Psychological Influences 25

Chapter Two
The Birth of an Organisation
The Political Motives and Social Background of the Membership in
Nottingham and Leicester 38

Chapter Three
Growth of the Pankhurst Autocracy and its Consequences 66

Chapter Four
Truce, New Horizons and the Expansion of Trade Unionism in Leicester 94

Chapter Five
The Return to Militancy and its Political, Economic and
Social Consequences 126

Conclusion
Themes and Issues Within the WSPU 156

Appendices
Reply to Malcolm MacDonald, 1907 (Letter from Alice) 168
Chronology of events within the East Midlands 169
WSPU Membership for Leicester for 1907–14 182
Some Impressions of Prison Life – HM Prison Holloway 183
Equity 185
TUC 187
Alice Hawkins's place of burial 188
Search for Suffragette descendents 189
LeicestHERday 190

ACKNOWLEDGEMENTS

I would like to thank, first and foremost, Ron Greenall and Rob Coll at the University of Leicester for their help and useful comments during the initial research. Also, I would like to thank the staff at the Leicestershire Records Office in Wigston, who were extremely helpful, Brian Lund for the use of the photos of Blaby Railway Station, Zoë Oughton for her original photos, Peter Barratt, Maureen Milgram Forrest and Jayne Pallett, my partner, for all their enthusiastic support, but especially Mrs Vera Barratt, granddaughter of Alice, who made all this possible by the loan of Alice's scrapbook.

Other acknowledgements made on behalf of all of us involved in the loving development of this book include:

Alan Forrest, editor

Nick Carter and Steve England from the *Leicester Mercury*

Kate Squire and David Harvey from BBC Radio Leicester

All of the descendents of Alice Hawkins and, in particular, Madge Kemp, Vera Barratt, Joan Nelson, Peter Barratt, Joanne Preston and Jim Beadman, who have held many of the private collections handed down through the generations

All of the trustees and staff of the LeicestHERday Trust

Members of the Leicester City Council Museums staff, including Sarah Levitt, Shriti Patel, Philip French and colleagues

Members of the Leicestershire County Council Museums staff, including Heather Broughton, Jess Jenkins, Philip Warren and colleagues

All of those who searched for ephemera and memorabilia, including the all-elusive search for the 1907 'Votes for Women' banner

Roger McKenzie, Regional Secretary of the TUC

Peter Crowe and Pat Robinson, Community KFAT Union

Gordon Smart and Gabi of the Footwear Benevolent Society

David Bolton, The Equity Shoes

County Record Office

Leicester Mercury Archives

FOREWORD

From Rt Hon Patricia Hewitt, MP Leicester West
Secretary of State for Health

*'One never notices
what has been done;
one can only see
what remains to be done.'*
Marie Curie, head of the physics laboratory
at the Sorbonne,
winner of the Nobel Prize for physics
(along with her husband)
in 1903 for their study of radiation.

LEGACY is what it is all about when you review the centenary years of 1907 to 2007 through the life of Alice Hawkins.

Alice campaigned for women's suffrage and the vote for women in 1907. In 2007, as a woman MP with a cabinet position, I am fortunate to represent all that Alice and her colleagues fought for, and more.

If Alice were alive today, what would she think of women in parliament and women as chief executives of private and public sector companies? Women worldwide making important decisions.

I think that she would be saying it was worth it. In 1907 and again in later years she broke the law to fight for a right she believed in.

Today, we are using the law to break down further barriers to women's aspirations across a wide range of achievements.

Only 30 years ago we passed into law both the Sex Discrimination Act (protecting the rights of men and women) and the Equal Pay Act.

In 2007 we need to review and monitor the gender pay gap that still exists. We need to continue raising women's expectations and make it easier for mothers and fathers to balance work and family. To reach the decision-making plateaux, we need to treat women of all ethnic origins and religions equally across the workplace. We need to raise women's skills and confidence.

Alice's story is inspirational. There are more barriers to bring down.

We can take pride in her achievements and look to make life even better today as part of her legacy to us.

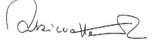

FOREWORD

Peter Barratt – Alice's great-grandson

In this day and age, when all political parties complain of voter apathy, it seems almost unbelievable that a hundred years ago the women of this country literally fought for that very basic human right…the right to vote.

My great-grandmother, Alice Hawkins, was but one of many women who campaigned for that right. A shoe machinist by trade and a strong socialist, Alice joined forces with women of all social backgrounds and all political persuasions, for never before were so many women united for a common cause.

For many women who campaigned as suffragettes, unfortunately their own valiant story has been lost over the mist of time. For Alice however, the story of her own personal fight to gain the right to vote has been kept alive and is as fresh today as it was a hundred years ago.

Cousins Vera, Madge, Joan, Norman and Eric, all grandchildren of Alice, are rightly proud of her achievements on the issue of women's rights and have kept the suffragette memorabilia and oral history within the family for later generations to see and remember.

But if it was not for the hundreds of hours of research undertaken by local historian Richard Whitmore, the memorabilia and history of Alice would have been but pieces in an incomplete jigsaw puzzle. The family owe a great debt of gratitude, therefore, to Richard for his authorative account of the women's struggle in Edwardian Leicester, and also to Maureen Milgram of the charity LeicestHERday for working so hard to achieve its publication.

But what memories do the grandchildren have of Alice, for even today she is still within living memory. They tell me she was a strong-willed, determined woman, who would often argue with the family in order to win her point of view. Alice was clearly a difficult woman to live with, but without those characteristics she would never have had the resolve to fight against the social inequalities of the day.

I often sit down with my mum Vera and her cousins Madge and Joan and ask them of their memories of Alice. Individually they tell me many stories, but collectively they always tell the same. They say that when they were young girls Alice said to them 'you must use your vote, we suffered for it'.

A message from all those years ago, just as true today.

INTRODUCTION

*'A man cannot feign a woman's feelings; he does not know
her wrongs; he wrongs her most himself. He is the Tyrant.'*
The Pioneer, 26 October 1833

The age between the Industrial Revolution and World War One is often seen as a period of emancipation of the urban and industrial classes. Indeed, historians have placed the emancipation of women of all social classes in the context of the growth of Britain as a politically democratic society. Yet although social historians have described in detail, and with a measure of sympathy, the plight of women and the campaign of the Women's Social and Political Union, they have tended to overlook the wealth of evidence found at a local level. Instead, a broad national picture has often been painted of women's fight for equality, which distracts from any real understanding of who these women were.

This view suggests that the fight for emancipation had little to do with ordinary women outside the capital and, instead, propagates the belief that only a small and privileged band of women were responsible for the militant struggle. The assumption that only wealthy women were involved in the militant campaign has led not only to the distortion of the WSPU membership, but it also neglects the significant contribution made by working-class women within it.

In reality, many thousands of nameless women, like Alice Hawkins, were prepared to endure the hardship of prison and ostracism within their community in the name of women's rights, and this is an important omission if we are to understand their ideas and motivations. For it is these women who invariably sought to solve the problems of housing, poverty and other social predicaments that occurred in their everyday lives.

The Leicester WSPU was almost certainly begun by working women as a response to their inferior positions within the workplace; they saw the vote as a method of achieving better wages and improved working conditions for women who needed to work to alleviate poverty within the family unit, rather than the sexual degradation created by the ideology of separate spheres and the double-standard morality of men.

Emmeline Pankhurst, founder of the Women's Social and Political Union in 1904.

But who were these women and what were the forces that shaped their lives? In order to address this question, it is necessary to investigate the social and economic backgrounds of these women and interrogate the forces that shaped them into becoming who they

MRS. PANKHURST.
HON. SECRETARY, NATIONAL WOMEN'S SOCIAL & POLITICAL UNION.
4, CLEMENT'S INN, W.C.

BY MARTIN JACOLETTE, SOUTH KENSINGTON.

were. Perhaps the most important of these was the world of work in the Leicester boot and shoe factories.

According to figures recorded in 1911, the amount of female shoe workers in Leicester increased dramatically in the factories around the town, while the large pockets of homeworkers in the surrounding areas remained the same. One third of the 33,000 workers, mostly women, engaged in the boot and shoe trade were still working outside the town. What these figures show is just how unimportant the old domestic system was to the new manufacturing process.

Consequently, there was a real increase in the proportion of women workers in the labour force, especially as machinists in closing – a practice which continued as the trade moved into the factory at the end of the 1890s. Around the town, female employment increased from 7,320 workers in 1891 to 8,791 in 1901. This amounted to an extra 41% between 1881 and 1911 and corresponded well to the overall 44% increase in the female population.

It was clearly economic and political factors that were so critical in prising the Leicester women from the received opinions of the social and cultural systems in which they worked and transformed them into their unique pattern of radical feminism. But how did their political diversity affect their relationship with other political groups and organisations, while at the same time keeping in mind the vertical problems of how middle-class women related to working-class women and their issues?

In Leicester, the Labour Party and Ramsay MacDonald should have been natural allies; after all, they could claim a common background, and while MacDonald was not entirely against the principle of votes for women he was appalled by WSPU militancy and often clashed with Alice Hawkins over political direction.

In the early years of the Leicester WSPU, Alice Hawkins, out from under the ever-watchful eye of Clement's Inn, had a liking for revolutionary socialism, and for some time she was allowed a free rein, but under the guidance of the leadership in London and the arrival of a paid organiser, Dorothy Pethick, she was exposed, however unwillingly, to other viewpoints and directions which meant that policy priorities often shifted. Consequently, it is here that the gap between her socialist ambitions and the goal of only seeking votes for women on a single platform can be found. For Alice, the policy of votes for women was an enabling issue that would allow all other reforms to stem from it, and from the start there was no other agenda to pursue or develop. Yet, more importantly, there were no other political objectives to suppress.

Alice Hawkins, founder of the Women's Social and Political Union in 1907. She was a life-long campaigner of women's issues and Labour politics.

13

However, by 1911 Alice Hawkins was once again allowed to pursue her real interests. During the truce of 1910 and 1911, Alice Hawkins and others from the Leicester WSPU undertook a lengthy campaign of recruiting more women into the local trade union movement. Inspired by the radical feminism of Christabel Pankhurst, these women, according to local trade union members, were now fighting a sex war with the men. In this brutal assessment of the women's intentions and motives, there lies a powerful combination of male logic and political assumptions that suggest these women were little more than troublemakers, bent on diverting the work of the union to make positive discriminations in their favour.

However, that view failed to fully assess their aims and goals and denied in any real manner the extent to which these women were exploited, both in the home and at work. But, in this case, to speak only of somebody as being a victim of exploitation and not as being oppressed because they were women fails to focus on the lives of ordinary women. It is important, therefore, not to look at women in terms of their political or social backgrounds, but at how they were being treated as women.

To some extent, Alice Hawkins more than understood this concept and attacked at every opportunity the reluctance of men to include women in all aspects of social and political life. By 1911 she was painfully conscious that the moment that had beckoned her was one to which her whole life had been pointing. Since she had joined the trade union movement, she had expected much and yet received little from her male colleagues. She had worked tirelessly on behalf of the women of Leicester, but little had come of this energy. Thus, when the negotiations had reached their final schism, the formation

During the process of industrialisation, many thousands of women found work within the new boot and shoe factories.

of an independent female union seemed to offer liberation from male hypocrisy and inertia.

But to what extent was Alice Hawkins's radicalism home-grown or developed by the Pankhurst experience? Or does a person's evolution demand that he or she be encompassed in a wider circle of experience and exposure to a more radical way of thinking? In some respects the answer is both, and the transformation that Alice Hawkins underwent as a suffragette certainly motivated her trade union activity, but only up to a point. Her work with the trade union movement was never fully left behind, and in some ways this attitude coloured the activity of the rest of the branch. Thus, while it might be prudent to ask if she was being influenced by the WSPU, it is certainly true that she influenced the WSPU, even if it was only at a local level.

In many respects, the Leicester suffragettes' fight for the vote was no different from any other well-documented group, like the Women's Freedom League and the London WSPU, who struggled for the right to political emancipation within the capital. Yet, to date, as it has been pointed out, little attention has been paid to the women who joined the organisation and remained outside the small band of women revolving around the Pankhursts in London. Their presence was no less important, and indeed they undoubtedly added to the WSPU's colour and make-up. Yet, more importantly, they were the sum of its character and strength, for, without the loyal supporters around the country, little could have been done to make the life of the politician difficult.

In countless towns and boroughs around Britain, local women harassed and harangued Cabinet Ministers and local MPs in the name of 'Votes For Women', and none more so than within Leicester. Indeed, between May 1907 and June 1914 nearly 50 incidents occurred. Herbert Asquith, Winston Churchill and Ramsay MacDonald all fell foul of this campaign. In common with the textile workers around the Lancashire cotton towns, the rise of a new type of industrial women worker made the area a potential breeding ground for recruits to the new and dynamic Women's Social and Political Union.

Outside London, thousands of quiet and respectable women like Alice Hawkins toiled out of the limelight, not only to raise substantial amounts of money for the cause by 'self-denial weeks', but also to put the question of women's suffrage at the top of the political agenda.

Often this was done against their natural instincts and political

Women working in a Leicester boot and shoe factory before World War One. This experience made them politically aware and militant.

persuasions. But, over the years, the policies of the WSPU did little to cement the support of the ILP and local trade unions, and often the hostility towards militant feminism would come from the rank and file of male employees on the shop floor and trade unionists seeking to restrict the use of cheap female labour. For them, the problem was manifestly twofold. Not only did women keep wages artificially low by supplying cheap labour, but they also occupied a job that could have been done by a man. They argued, with some justification, that while some households received two wages when both the husband and wife worked, many households received none when the husband could not find work. On this point the solution was clear: the priority of work must fall to the man and then all households might, at least, receive one wage, and then the union might have a claim to argue for a higher rate as the men have wives and children to support.

It was on this problem of male hostility towards women workers within the trade union movement that the first suggestions of a Leicester suffragette movement were uncovered in an unexpected way. In an extensive history of the National Union of Boot and Shoe Operatives, Alan Fox outlined the rise and consequent struggle of a section of working women within the union, who not only strove to gain recognition for their grievances, but also fought to achieve the unthinkable goal of equal pay and better working conditions for all working women. These women, while faced with personal rejection and even ridicule, felt confident enough to start their own independent union in 1911. But something of the attitude of the men within the boot and shoe union can be seen in the irrelevance Alan Fox puts upon the women's movement at that time. Of course, while accepting the women's union had some justification and that it was not entirely connected with a few fanatics engaged in a sex war against all men, he concluded that it was merely a nuisance, or, at best, a sideshow that diverted attention away from the union's major concern of attaining higher wages for the men so they could keep their wives and children in reasonable conditions.

In some respects, while Alan Fox's assumption that the women's agitation within Leicester's boot and shoe industry needed to be seen against the backdrop of the wider suffragette movement was correct, he somewhat missed the point when he suggested that these women were influenced by a wider pattern of agitation rather than being an important part of it. But it is worth noting that trade union militancy within these women originally fed suffrage expectations; however, suffragette activity led to a more dynamic trade union militancy around 1911. The exceptional militancy of the Leicester women was largely due to the dynamic personalities of some of the local women, like Alice Hawkins, Bertha Clark and Lizzie Willson. Equally important was the encouragement and open support of many male workers within the radical concept of co-op manufacture. Their radicalism was essentially a local phenomenon and was generated from inside the Labour movement.

While this book is primarily about Alice Hawkins, it could not be told without a wider reference to the other women within the Leicester WSPU and some parts need to be given over to them. Secondly, it would be difficult to assess Alice Hawkins and her role as a suffragette without reference to the group as a whole. For, while she was able to shape their outlook, they too could do the same for her, and one aspect of her personality was her development of radical feminism.

But what was radical feminism at this time and precisely how are these labels measured? It is widely accepted that the problem of defining meaning within a historical context is difficult, and there is a need to devise and ground a conception of truth which will be as adequate to the new historical modes of knowing as they were seen in their own time; however, they also need to include a synthesis between meaning and understanding, both of which are seen by later generations as relevant, and must link up to the way in which all people increasingly experience their lives. Thus, when trying to predetermine what constituted radical feminism in Alice Hawkins and others at the turn of the 20th century there is a difficulty, because the definition of radical feminism not only changed as the century progressed, but it also changed between different people and different ideologies. Indeed, some of the ambiguity in the term stems from the fact that it was used in different, but partially overlapping, ways.

For example, before World War One there were conflicting differences of opinion in the approach to feminism, as defined by early radicals like Alice Hawkins and later Christabel Pankhurst. For Alice Hawkins, her radicalism was a traditional radical feminism for the turn of the century and really only sought to demand access into a world controlled by men by demanding equal rights at work, equal rights in education and, of course, the vote. In some ways this might also be seen as the classic proletariat view espoused by a male political organisation, but the demands for reform made by Alice Hawkins appear to reflect her experiences within the workplace. She neither had the leisure nor the education to define her feminism

Emmeline Pankhurst.

around her biology. Yet that does not mean to say that the problems of contraception and family allowances were beyond her scope, it had more to do with the fact that the Labour movement had yet to define its policy on such matters.

However, the WSPU was to give Alice Hawkins an altogether different approach. She was forced into the political debate that now focused on women's biological and sexual oppression. This 'new feminism' insisted on a real equality; this not only meant challenging a male dominated culture, but it also meant recognising the specific predicaments of women. Not only was the new agenda demanding better protection for women at work, but it also sought to take command of birth control, abortion and sexual freedom from male exploitation. At the heart of the matter, militancy lay principally in showing new ways of being a woman, and its rhetoric appealed directly to the new Edwardian woman. Obviously this was more than just a doctrine of equal rights for women; at its best it set out to redefine a woman's role, not only in the home but also in the wider social, economic and political sphere of men.

Although radical feminism articulated the way in which women could see themselves, it nevertheless blurred the real contradictions within the movement. At no point could it achieve, in real terms, the possibility of change for the housewife or the exploited women at work.

As a growing number of working women like Alice Hawkins became more class-conscious, organised and militant, they increasingly saw themselves shaped by the reproductive process rather than by the rounded needs of human personality. This is an important key to understanding the persistence of feminist agitation in that it lies in analysing not only the social and economic developments of the 19th century, but the ideological developments as well.

Adela Pankhurst.

Throughout the period, the leadership of the WSPU consistently provided the necessary ideologues to help women like Alice understand their own experiences and the aims and tasks of the struggle. The movement's leadership itself learnt to organise the union and mastered the art, at least in the early years, to control and set the political and sexual agenda by dictating popular opinion among many women. Indeed, as late as 1913 Emmeline Pankhurst proclaimed in a speech that prostitution was a metaphor of the position of all women and that 'it was, perhaps, the main reason for militancy'.

The Pankhursts understood only too well that new theoretical perceptions of what women could and should be would only be worked out by creating and developing a parallel view of a woman's sphere of influence. By 1912 they had managed, through Christabel's views on male double standards, to develop a scientific breadth and a theoretical depth that would give many middle-class women the courage to leave home in search of a new identity. Indeed, such was the Pankhursts' influence that the movement brought into prominence many personalities, who made their mark in the chronicles of women's thought. Needless to say, the age itself generated the need for such personalities, and, despite the obvious differences in gender, the metaphor is still the same as Hegal's maxim that 'the great man of the age is the one who can put into words the will of his age'. However, they were not individuals prone to penis envy, battling against the immovable bastions of male privilege, they were women who refused to be defined essentially in terms of their biology and would no longer consent to be passive victims of male sexual tyranny.

Christabel Pankhurst.

However, there are problems of overgeneralisation; early feminists not only had to fight the concept that they were violating God's nature of women, but also had to deal with clergymen interrupting women's rights meetings. While this might have been true in some places, it certainly was not true of women's meetings in Leicester; the Church actively supported the suffrage movement and forged links with them through organisations like the Church League for Women's Suffrage.[1] Here, WSPU members like Dorothy Pethick encompassed both worlds with equal commitment, and, indeed, she was matched with equal passion from church leaders and clergymen alike. Unfortunately, much of this solidarity was to be lost in the eruption of militancy after 1912, and relationships were strained to breaking point when churches were attacked and burned down.

For Alice Hawkins, there was another aspect to her life that were just as important as her radical feminism, and that was her class or social status. For example, Alice Hawkins maintained a working-class concept of herself all her life, and to some degree she was right, but it is important to bear in mind that there was a high degree of class-consciousness throughout the female workforce of Leicester, and she was undoubtedly influenced by this. Almost from the start, the process of mechanisation within the boot and shoe trade created a new set of political ambitions within its workforce that centred on the demand for legislative control of wages and terms of employment. As a consequence, throughout the East Midlands working women, alongside their male colleagues, were flexing their industrial muscles in tandem with trade union action.

There were, of course, deep structural divisions within the working class itself that prevented the development of a widespread, cohesive class-consciousness, which in turn restricted the development of working-class politics at this time. Consequently, it was from the skilled and unionised craftsmen that the ILP and other political organisations drew the majority of their working-class support. Without doubt, Alice Hawkins was part of this movement, and as such presented herself to the world as a manifestation of the qualities and characteristics valued by this group.

Alice's story is important in that it constructs a picture of an individual's political convictions and how it impacted on her personal behaviour. Of course, it might well be argued that Alice's commitment to a political organisation such as the WSPU had little to do with personality characteristics and more to do with convictions based on material interests determined by class considerations. But much of the evidence suggests that personality and individual characteristics had much to do with how the Leicester WSPU developed and behaved.

This is all the more important when it is realised that there was frequently an interaction between the local and national organisations, and often the strength and reliability of a member's involvement was generally determined by the response of the leadership in London. But, equally, the leadership's involvement in the struggle cannot be fully understood without reference to the wider organisation, and only when we see their decisions being taken in the light of local pressures and local women like Alice Hawkins can we fully understand the dynamics that underpinned the Women's Social and Political Union. The local story of Alice Hawkins is, then, crucial to our understanding of the organisation.

Finally, the process of collecting and collating material for this book was surprisingly difficult, in that much of the material was hidden from view and had to be found. None of the national archives consulted held records that directly related to Leicester. Secondly, previous researchers had sought in vain for these women among the middle classes, when, in reality, they were initially to be found in the factories and workshops engaged in boot and shoe manufacture.

Consequently, from this unique starting point it was a relatively simple matter of advertising in the regional papers for local information. However, what was to turn up surpassed all expectations when the granddaughter of Alice Hawkins, one of Leicester's leading members, produced her scrapbook.

From this it was possible to investigate the rich source of information to be found in local newspapers, as all the publications in Leicester considered the local suffragettes to be of such worth as to document their progress from 1907 to 1914. Within the pages of these newspapers were not only accounts of their meetings but also their letters and interviews with reporters. Further, they were considered to be of such newsworthy merit that many other commentators felt the need to add to the rich flow of information.

Sadly, after the campaign was wound up in 1914, few of these women thought themselves important enough to record or document their group in any real detail. It appeared that these women left little, if any, significant evidence regarding their activities within the organisation. Of course, the fact that in later years the

Mrs Barrett, the granddaughter of Alice Hawkins, outside the Equity boot and shoe co-operative, the cradle of the Leicester suffragette movement.

The decorative lintel over the door of the Equity.

21

Sylvia Pankhurst.

organisation became secretive and little was written down only hampered the investigation further.

As it has already been pointed out, a detailed search of all the local newspapers was needed, and it was ultimately possible to use media accounts as evidence regarding incidents and disorder. Without doubt, this was useful, despite the fact that the selection of newsworthy material was often not only distorted to fit a stereotypical image demanded by their readers, but was also frequently used to promote the newspaper's own particular brand of social remedies when dealing with political agitation and public disorder, and none more so than the *Leicester Mercury* where any political protest was seen as an infringement of Liberal democracy. While, on the other hand, a relatively short-lived socialist newspaper, *The Pioneer*, considered the movement to be of such interest that it recorded in some detail the early years of the WSPU within the town.

But, more importantly, regional newspapers were able to supply a list of names of the many activists who could be tracked down later by other means – notably local directories, advertising in local newspapers and by making appeals on local radio stations. For married women this task was somewhat easier, for they had the names of their husbands and they could often be found in local directories like *White's* and *Kelly's*. However, by collating the meagre evidence from local directories and by placing their residences within a local context it was possible to determine social class, or at least the social class of their husbands or fathers.

Alice was awarded this medal for going to prison for the cause. The 1910 ribbon was given to Alice for her part in the demonstration that became known as Black Friday.

The prison gates were worn by those who had suffered imprisonment.

Of course, not all questions could be answered from newspaper articles, but they were a good pointer to other source materials, like the Leicester Police Watch Committee reports and the archives in the Fawcett Library in London. Access to these files would have been pointless without knowing the names of the people involved, as much of the information contained in the library would name names, but, more often than not, not mention localities.

There were, of course, secondary sources like memoirs, newsletters, newspapers and books written by the suffragettes, like Sylvia Pankhurst's *The Suffragette Movement*, which proved to be of value. But, of course, the newspapers like *The Suffragette* and *Votes For Women* were always meant as vehicles for propaganda and unashamedly presented a biased view, even at the time. For, without doubt, they often only contained what the leadership deemed fit for public consumption and often left out any facts that were deemed damning to the organisation.

Alice Hawkins's WSPU sash.

City of Leicester
ALICE HAWKINS
1863 - 1946
Leader of the women's
suffrage movement
in Leicester
Worked for many years
at Equity Shoes

The blue plaque on the wall of the Equity, remembering Alice Hawkins.

Yet this does not render them totally useless, as the bias itself has historical relevance in that it informs the reader of the ways in which individuals and, indeed, social groups like the WSPU assimilated and interpreted their own experience, and this is at the heart of our own political culture. Further, they are important source documents for the simple fact that they recorded political and social events as they unfolded, and it is this accumulation of experience that shaped and influenced their lives. Moreover, *Votes For Women* contained many listings of demonstrations and gatherings that not only helped signpost the growth of the movement but also gave an indication of what to look for in other source documents.

For example, when it was known that the suffragettes conducted a demonstration with several arrests, it is a relatively small matter to check the provincial press reports for local women who had been arrested, and from that it was possible to locate their ages, occupations and addresses. But, more importantly, it was feasible to note their levels of activity and, indeed, their level of commitment to the cause.

Note

1   This organisation was formed in December 1909 and sought to promote the moral, social and industrial well being of the community.

A picture postcard from Alice Hawkins's scrapbook.

THE WORKER'S HUSBAND.

Lady Canvasser. **Have you a vote, Mr. Brown?**
Loafer. **'Course I got a vote, and shall have so long as my wife takes in washing.**

Chapter One
Radical Traditions and Psychological Influences

'Freedom lies in being bold'
Robert Frost

Alice Hawkins was born into a world of poverty and deprivation in Stafford on 4 March 1863 and moved to Leicester sometime in her early youth to begin work in the new boot and shoe factories. These were springing up around the town and, like many other women workers within the boot and shoe industry, Alice had been consistently introduced to radical working-class politics, with the result that by the 1890s she was deeply involved in the two most prominent working-class organisations within the town, notably the infant Labour Party and the comparatively successful Women's Co-operative Guild. It was within these groups that women not only fought for a realistic minimum wage, but also campaigned to improve working conditions for thousands of Leicester women; it is against this background that Alice Hawkins needs to be seen and understood, for without an understanding of the forces and influences that shaped her life it would be difficult to understand the woman.

For some years it was always assumed that Alice Hawkins was Leicester's only working-class suffragette, but although we now know that to be wrong – the branch had a high percentage of working women – Alice Hawkins was, nevertheless, one of the most influential members within the local movement. Schooled in the politics of radical trade union and scorned by her fellow trade unionists for being too radical, she had come to see that the struggle for the vote was her best option for improving low wages and poor working conditions for thousands of working women in Leicester.

As a consequence of her actions and political ideology, the local Women's Social and Political Union was formed in April 1907, and at her insistence working women throughout the East Midlands not only took an active part in the campaigns of the WSPU, but they also helped motivate and direct policies on a regional level. Indeed, none were more suited to the work, for they were often better able to understand the needs and grievances of working women than the leadership in London.

In lofty matters such as those, the Women's Co-operative Guild proved more than adept at promoting political issues of worthy note. Indeed, not only did the socialist Tom Mann find a hearty welcome when he came to talk on syndicalism, but when the Equity Shoes Women's Guild met for the first time on 19 February 1896 Mrs Dring of Lincoln read a paper entitled '*The Evils of Homework For Women*'. More importantly, as early as 1893 it had been decided among the Guild women to promote a national appeal to raise a motion in favour of women's suffrage. As a result of this drive, 2,200 signatures were collected nationally in support of the motion that was framed as 'the political enfranchisement of women is a part of that social justice which we, with all other social reformers, are zealously striving for'.

It was primarily because of this involvement in Labour politics and industrial issues that the Women's Co-operative Guild, drawing on female employees like Alice Hawkins within the boot and shoe industry, could be seen as the cradle of the Leicester suffragette movement, in that its members were both working class and socialists. The hosiery trade also saw women giving tacit support to socialist-inspired leadership within the Leicester Amalgamated Hosiery Union. Therefore, not for the first time, working women were attempting to relate their industrial struggles to a change in their political status.

For Alice Hawkins, during the 1890s, the vote and improved working conditions were intrinsically bound together, and she consistently argued that one could not be achieved without the other. Consequently, unlike the Women's Co-operative Guild in Northampton, who tended to absent themselves from national

The Equity Shoes, as a forward thinking employer, introduced an education room for the benefit of their staff.

issues, the Leicester women played a major role in the campaigns of the Guild, promoting both social and industrial issues. For example, after Mrs Abbott of Tunbridge Wells broached the question of the new Poor Law in 1894, Leicester women like Mrs Lowe and Mrs Barnes, who both later joined the WSPU, successfully sought to be elected as Poor Law Guardians. Indeed, given its interest in the problems of women and children, it was natural that much of the Guild's attention should centre upon the new Poor Law.

The Leicester Women's Co-operative Guild was formed in Leicester in 1890 and almost from the start played an important role in ordinary women's lives. Not only did it give them a forum in which they could discuss the issues and problems that directly affected them, but it also allowed them, as D.H. Lawrence so eloquently puts it in *Sons and Lovers*, to 'look at their homes, at the conditions of their own lives, and find fault'.

On this point, it is important to remember that the Women's Guild in the North of England provided one of the most important sources for women's suffrage before the formation of the WSPU in the larger textile areas like Bury, Burnley and Manchester, and in this respect Leicester proved to be no exception as many women were introduced to radical feminism alongside many famous non-militant suffragists like Mrs Ashworth and Mrs Bury, a mill worker from Darwen. These women often frequented meetings within the town, and so intense were some of these debates that Mrs Bury, attending her first assembly in 1895, declared:

> 'It was a revelation…At the close of the meeting I felt as I imagined a warhorse must feel when he hears the beat of drums. What I saw and heard at Leicester changed the whole of my life for the next few years.'

As a result, this long-established radical feminism was to have two major repercussions within the Labour movement. Firstly, it was to colour the activities of working women within the trade union movement as it brought into sharp relief the need for all trade unionists, whether male or female, to win the vote. And secondly, it was to demonstrate to working women the futility of expecting both help and support from their male colleagues. As one Leicester woman lamented in 1890, 'There are many things in connection with the labour of women in factories which require the attention of trade unions.'

Therefore, almost from the start, the fight for recognition of women's concerns appeared to be an uphill struggle. Indeed, many male trade unionists within the footwear industry not only brought pressure to bear on young women to conform to official union policy, but also continually objected to married women working in the industry at all.

A major debate raged through the pages of the *Leicester Mercury* in 1913, as men complained that women were taking jobs that men could do. They also suggested, with some credibility, that it was unfair for some families to take home two wage packets in times of high unemployment. As a result of this dogmatic male intransigence, the relationship between the sexes in Leicester deteriorated further and reflected the hostility of 1911 when open war broke out.

At the root of this problem was the lack of male support for female issues, and when Alice Hawkins and Lizzie Willson, with other women employees within the boot and shoe industry, sought to form a breakaway union in November 1911, it broke out into open warfare.

In Charnwood, the Anchor Co-operative works were accused by the female employees of taking coercive measures against female workers when both the Co-operative and the union not only fined two male trade unionists for speaking at a women's meeting, but also forced the women, on the pain of dismissal, back into the NUBSO against their will. As Alan Fox pointed out in *A History of the National Union of Boot and Shoe Operatives, 1874–1957,*

'This uneasy relationship between the sexes needs to be seen against the background of the militant suffrage movement if its full significance is to be realised…By 1910 what had begun as a modest and respectable movement by mainly middle-class women for certain limited suffrage rights, had developed into

The Anchor Boot and Shoe Co-operative factory.

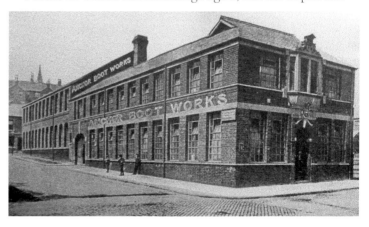

a women's rebellion against the inferiority of women's status and the limitations on their opportunities for self-fulfilment.'

However, their experiences within the workplace and their subjective position within the home were also their teachers, and by 1907 evidence suggests that many Leicester women were at the fore of local politics and trade unions. Though while not normally in a position to dominate and set local agendas, they were often able to influence and promote issues that concerned them.

This was because, while there was a measure of radical feminism within the trade union movement, there was also a positive reaction to anti-feminism by the Left, and there was much condemnation of male trade unionists who refused to involve themselves in women's issues.

Indeed, trade unionism in Leicester was more important than in other shoe-manufacturing centres. In 1888 the Leicester NUBSO membership stood at well over 6,000. This represented one trade unionist to every 2.4 workers in the Leicester boot and shoe trade by 1891. Consequently, it is possible to argue that employees in Leicester were far more radical than in other areas and, therefore, led by example. Moreover, despite the fact that many women found it difficult to identify with a masculine milieu of local trade unionism, in many ways the men still supplied radical role models that women could follow and aspire to.

Thus, by the end of 1907 the formation of the WSPU in Leicester was, for Alice Hawkins, an opportunity to have a real voice in the world, and because of local conditions, and the fact that each person's political activities are channelled by the way in which they conceptualise and anticipate their needs, Alice's priorities and consequently her strategies were bound to be different from those in London. At first, many Leicester women attempted to explore and correct the problems as they saw them in their own lives, and, as a result, the WSPU within the town was often seen by these women as a vehicle to promote social and economic change within their immediate environment.

This is an important point, and often this view was at odds with the Pankhursts' conception of what the WSPU should be. Indeed, the wider picture visualised by the Pankhursts in London had little reality in Leicester, and, quite often, their strategies and political ambitions meant very little to women on the shop floor and within the home.

In contrast, the local women often wanted the WSPU to offer

change at a local level and to work hand-in-hand with other political organisations. But all this was not to happen. From 1908 onwards, independence and democracy within the WSPU were to be sacrificed at the Pankhursts' altar of autocratic control. Instead, local issues, whatever they were, were not allowed to cloud the issue of votes for women, and all members, regardless of their past and political experience, were to conform without question.

In Leicester the WSPU was begun primarily by working-class women for working-class motives and had come about as a direct consequence of a faltering campaign waged by constitutional suffragists, both in Leicester and elsewhere.

By the end of the 19th century, despite unrelenting pressure applied by such stalwarts as Millicent Fawcett, Ada Nield Chew, Elizabeth Garrett Anderson and Lydia Becker, the suffrage crusade had made little headway in the 20 years between 1870 and 1890. In truth, the respectable facade that was 'sensible, patient and undeviating sanguine' had always been met by stoic intransigence on the part of Liberal ministers, who believed, as 19th-century politicians once thought of working men, that to enfranchise women would be a further leap in the dark.

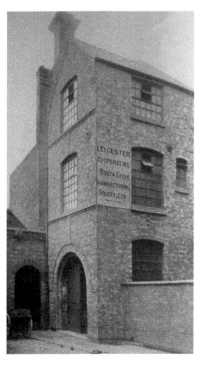

The first Equity boot and shoe co-operative factory on Friars Causeway. This was situated on Braunstone Gate, around the corner from Western Road, Leicester.

Instead, they 'found their sentiment in their womenfolk encased in their crinolines' and thought that a woman's place was not only in the home, but was also in a social position that was economically dependent upon a man. Consequently, the problems facing the constitutionalists in the 1880s went far deeper than just enfranchising women; it struck at the very heart of women's position in society. To accord women equality was not only politically dangerous, it was also a shift in their legal and economic status. Indeed, what chance had the annual Women's Suffrage Bill, 'with its threadbare arguments and antique air, of enlisting support and commanding attention?' The answer, quite simply, was none at all. To all intents and purposes, the campaign, in the face of determined male prejudice, had all but ground to a dignified halt.

However, the struggle for women's rights in industry had produced a new breed of radical women that would take up the cudgels of the women's movement as the new century dawned, and in Leicester women like Miss Bertha Clark, Mrs Lowe (wife of a local Labour Councillor) and Mrs Alice Hawkins had long been active members of the NUBSO and had vigorously campaigned to improve working conditions within the industry. As an active socialist and an exponent of the co-operative ideal, Alice Hawkins had begun work in the 1880s at the age of 13 as a machinist in the newly-founded Co-operative factory, Equity Boot and Shoe Co-operative, on Friar's Causeway. Instilled with the ideas and principles of socialism, she joined the infant ILP in 1892, where she and her husband, Alfred, energetically sought to make female suffrage a real issue. Indeed, as early as 1895, under the auspices of the ILP's Women's Auxiliary, Alice Hawkins and others had often lamented the fact that under the present system of parliamentary representation, where one sex had no vote, women of all classes were, in reality, political nonentities.

Keir Hardie, first Labour MP and supporter of the WSPU in its early years.

This inequality inflamed their sense of political injustice, and they vehemently argued that in order to give women an interest in social questions of the day, they not only needed a direct stake in the political system, but, more importantly, they had to give them the power to deal directly with social and political problems as they arose. Clearly these women had an interest in the suffrage question long before the Pankhursts had brought it to the fore. But the question facing working-class women before 1904 was: by which route would they press their case?

That question was, for Alice Hawkins and other militant trade unionist women, simple to answer: they believed that their best chance lay with the up-and-coming infant ILP, despite the fact that the ILP had always been ambivalent on the question of women's suffrage.

On the other hand, members like Keir Hardie had always supported female suffrage as a matter of principle. However, to many influential policy makers within the Labour movement, the question was beyond the objectives of trade unions and the ILP. They sought to strengthen male workers' wage claims in the belief that it was the man's duty to provide for the woman, a tradition that can be traced back to the 1880s.

In 1902, confronted with indifference from her male colleagues, anger and frustration led one Leicester female commentator to note that the question of female suffrage was always cropping up like a poor relation that was waiting pathetically and patiently for wider recognition. These militant women were now prepared to work on the issue of votes for women outside the normal constraints of the ILP and the trade union movement, and rejected the slow but good work done by the Women's Co-operative Guild. Paradoxically, before the formation of the WSPU in Leicester, some women,

The Equity boot and shoe co-operative factory on Western Road. This building was built in 1898 and is still trading as a co-op.

including Alice Hawkins and Mrs Barnes, helped form what was to become the Women's Labour League in April 1906. This organisation was formed in Leicester after Mrs Ramsay MacDonald, Mrs Banton, Mrs Cox and Mrs Edith Barnes returned home from a WLL meeting in London and organised the first meeting at the home of Mrs Gilbert, of 72 Sparkenhoe Street. Immediately, the new Leicester branch received support from the Leicester MP, Mr Thomasson, and the Liberal, Sir John Rolleston.

At no point was this to be a women's wing of the Labour Party. Rather, it was to be an independent women's organisation that sought to advance and protect the industrial interests of all working women in much the same way that the Women's Co-operative Guild sought to protect and advance women's issues elsewhere. As Ramsay MacDonald later wrote:

> 'Invitations are being sent out to all Labour Party members of Parliament and candidates asking them to pass them on to their wives and other women supporters, to secretaries of affiliated trade unions with women members, and to socialist societies, asking them to pass on the invitations to women members likely to be able to attend.'

Initially, the idea to form the organisation was Mrs Margaret MacDonald's, and it was one of her most cherished projects, though undoubtedly the development of this group had been prompted by the success of the WSPU's campaign in the North of England.

According to both Sylvia Pankhurst and Keir Hardie, the ILP sought to stem the influx of working women into the Pankhursts' organisation by a recruitment drive of its own, and by July 1906 the local WLL was denouncing the tactics of the WSPU in London in favour of a more measured approach and appealed to working women to join the organisation with the message that 'Those women who think the main value of the vote is to readjust certain laws that tell hardly against their sex are profoundly mistaken.'

In the end, the formation of the WLL and its affiliation to the ILP was not enough to satisfy the radical demands of some of these women, and both Mrs Barnes and Alice Hawkins turned their backs on the organisation, helping to form the Leicester branch of the WSPU almost a year later.

As may be deduced by the desertion of some of these women from the WLL, however well intentioned these movements were, they lacked the fire and dynamism that the WSPU would later bring to the women of Leicester. Consequently, by 1904 local radical female trade unionists had come to realise that little had been done, or would be done, without drastic measures being taken to secure them the vote.

In Leicester, almost from the outset of their participation within local politics in the 1890s, it was clear that there would be little support within any political party for female suffrage. Of course, Ramsay MacDonald always maintained that he was in favour of the move, and in 1902 the Leicester ILP supported a petition in favour of giving votes to women on the same terms as men.

In reality, these acts of solidarity were little more than window dressing. Indeed, evidence from more local organisations like the trades council suggests that opposition was as rigid as ever. In response to a petition from Leeds, sponsored by Mr Allen Gee, to support a female franchise, Mr Lowe, a member of the no. 2 Branch of the NUBSO, summed up the feelings of the council when he maintained that the time was not yet ripe for women to have the vote. The petition was marginally rejected by 110 votes to 103.

As a result, within this climate of stagnation and frustration, the birth of militancy was surely inevitable. Radical women trade unionists' hopes and ambitions would not have allowed them to accept anything less. This frustration was further compounded when Mr Allen Gee's motion (that women be franchised on the same terms as men) was defeated in the Trade Union Congress. For many, this was a bitter blow. Instead, they contended that any measure, however limited, would be better than nothing and to object to the

Ramsay MacDonald, MP for Leicester. He went on to become the Labour Party's first Prime Minister.

Margaret MacDonald, wife of Ramsay MacDonald. She formed the Women's Labour League in 1906 to try and prevent women leaving the Labour Party in favour of the WSPU.

Oppposite: An early votes for women banner.

motion on the grounds that only propertied women would benefit was nonsense.

In the end, this impasse was broken in Manchester by what was, to all intents and purposes, a middle-class family committed to working-class machinations within the confines of the infant ILP. These tenacious women had both the personality and oratorical genius that would breathe life into a new movement and, although Christabel Pankhurst would later grow increasingly dissatisfied with the stance of many of the ILP's views on women's suffrage, this unique household would have the power to win over the hearts and minds of many women who were still emotionally and intellectually bound to socialism and the ILP.

This new organisation, the Women's Social and Political Union, was founded in Manchester in October 1903, and its policies would be in all respects identical to those of the Independent Labour Party. Consequently, it was suggested that the organisation be called the Women's Labour Representation Committee.

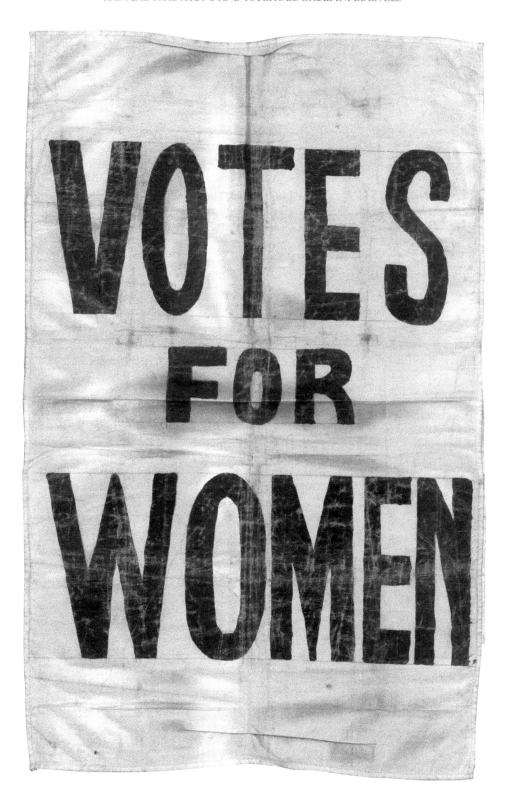

Unfortunately, Christabel Pankhurst was not present at this first meeting, and when later told of the proposed name she protested strongly that it was not possible. Her new-found friends, Miss Gore-Booth and Miss Roper, had planned another committee with just this name in mind. Shocked and hurt at her daughter's disapproval, Mrs Pankhurst caved in to Christabel's suggestion and renamed the group the Women's Social and Political Union, thus:

> 'The next day a few women, mostly working-class ILP supporters, arrived at 62 Nelson Street and within half an hour the Women's Social and Political Union was in business.'

Consequently, the WSPU was to bring to the women of Leicester a promise of active agitation that had hitherto been lacking within the trade union movement in Leicester, and, when a campaign against Government ministers began, they were wholeheartedly behind the move.

Opposite: Postcard from Alice Hawkins's scrapbook.

Chapter Two

The Birth of an Organisation

The Political Motives and Social Background of the Membership

'I want to be something so much worthier than a doll in the doll's house.'
Charles Dickens, *Mutual Friends*

It is not always easy to understand the motives and ambitions of women like Alice Hawkins, who formed a branch of the Leicester Women's Social and Political Union in 1907. However, it is important to bear in mind that in Leicester, as with elsewhere, the formation of the branch was intrinsically bound up in Labour politics and the women's trade union movement.

For example, on average, the number of socialists found within the WSPU across the East Midlands was relatively low, while in Leicester they were predominantly high. Since the Liberal middle class was trying to gain power within the wider union at large, the Leicester group becomes of historical importance.

These women had not only been deeply involved in the formation of the Leicester Labour Party, but they had also helped to form the Women's Labour League in 1906 and the Clarion Cycle Club. This club was unique in its day and, although the Clarion vans carried its socialist message far and wide, its politics were something that the average working man and women could understand.

Indeed, it was through the pages of its official organ, *The Clarion*, that these local women had been introduced to Christabel Pankhurst's views on female suffrage. In fact, Christabel had made much use of *The Clarion's* popular appeal to publicise the WSPU's policies and views. Consequently, when she approached Leicester's Trades Council Executive Committee to come and speak to its members, she was accepted without delay and arrived in Leicester on 18 July 1905.

Although the Leicester branch of the WSPU would not be started until 1907, she still found a willing audience who held convictions that were passionate and strong. Indeed, many of these women genuinely wanted freedom and equality for all women and deeply sympathised with the poor and oppressed, and given their ILP and trade union background these Leicester women clearly believed that their role as future suffragettes would be to promote equality in the workplace and to champion industrial questions with as much vigour as they could muster.

At first, Christabel really didn't have a problem with this view, and the Pankhursts in London appeared more than happy to allow new branches to pursue whatever local agenda they might choose, provided that it bowed to Pankhurst authority and did not question the dictates of WSPU strategy. At no point could they call into question the methods of the leadership in seeking votes for

Chas D. Drysdale. The Clarion Vanner.

The Clarion Van.
This was an effective way
in which to propagate
socialist ideas.

women. As Sylvia Pankhurst later recalled, all branches were built along democratic lines, even if the organisation itself was undemocratic.

They could elect their own officers and committees and were wholly independent of the headquarters, paying no fixed fees or dues (although fundraising was more than expected), and were only bound to Clement's Inn by sympathy to its policy of achieving votes for women.

Yet, by 1907 the autonomy enjoyed by the local branches was to be a source of division and dissent within the organisation, culminating in Mrs Billington-Greig and Mrs Despard leaving to form their own organisation, the Women's Freedom League. Sadly, the root causes are now unclear, but the crisis came to a head during the summer of 1907 when Mrs Billington-Greig, encouraged by a spirit of independence that was sweeping WSPU organisations in the north, sought to strengthen the local branches' independence by bringing them under the control of a regional council, the details of which have since been lost. However, the move to sever local branches from the Pankhursts in London was seen as a direct challenge to their authority and was prevented by removing all members who could not be relied upon to follow Christabel Pankhurst's orders without question.

Teresa Billington-Greig.

After 1906, due in part to the dynamic intervention of the WSPU in London and their subsequent publicity, there was a rapid and spontaneous growth of WSPU branches around the country. This was a period of unprecedented expansion, and by February 1907 not only did the union employ nine paid organisers, but £2,959 had been collected during its first fiscal year. This growth rate was set to continue, and during the financial year of 1908–09 its income was three times that of 1907–08. Nearly £3,500 had been spent on the hiring of halls alone, and the number of paid organisers had more than doubled to nearly 30 full-time officials.

Building on their initial success within the capital, paid organisers moved into the shire counties with the express purpose of mobilising as many women as possible. As a result, in most industrial centres around the Midlands many diverse groups of women, for different reasons, came together and formed, what was to be, the rank and file of provincial members. In some towns, notably Leicester, this new organisation gave working-class women a radical outlet for their anger and frustration as well as an instrument by which they could try to make substantial economic, social and political gains. Indeed, the participation of working women within this branch appeared to be unusually high. This is a pivotal point, as other local groups like Nottingham and Northampton branches took on the more usual form of middle-class suffragettes – dipping a tentative toe into the murky waters of radical feminism. This difference is all the more striking when it is remembered that both Leicester and Northampton had similar patterns of development, and both towns contained large numbers of women who worked within the boot and shoe industry. But, whereas Leicester could be looked upon as having radical and forward-thinking women, Northampton could not.

For while the Leicester women were able to become radicalised in the co-op movement and through trade union activity, this radicalisation was not transmitted to the women of Northamptonshire in the same way. There, trade union activity was a purely male preserve, and the local co-operative movement,

Mrs Despard, one of the founders of the Women's Freedom League.

because it was heavily controlled by the male co-operators, lacked the dynamism of their Leicester cousins. Instead, the WSPU, when it began its recruiting drive in Northampton during 1908 and 1909, succeeded in only recruiting middle-class women.

The decision to form the Leicester branch appears to have been made by Alice Hawkins some time in early 1907, after Mrs Billington-Greig, Mrs Cobden-Saunderson[1] and Miss Annie Kenny arrived at the Shoe Trade Hall in St James Street to talk about their recent experiences in prison. Each had suffered arrest and imprisonment for protesting outside Parliament in 1906 and, as part of WSPU policy, toured trades councils relating their story. It was in this manner that the WSPU once again came to Leicester, but this time what six Leicester working-class women, Alice Hawkins, Miss Wells, Miss Knight, Mrs Catlin, Mrs Lowe and Mrs Edith Barnes,[2] saw and heard at this meeting prompted them to travel to London in February to attend a Women's Parliament organised by the WSPU in Caxton Hall, the day before the State Opening of Parliament.[3] This was the first time that the Leicester women took part in WSPU demonstrations within the capital. However, their introduction to this new form of radicalism proved a costly affair in terms of lost wages and lost jobs.

The Women's Freedom League demonstrating outside the House of Commons. This lonely vigil continued for a number of months.

Ironically, the constitutionalists in the National Union of Women's Suffrage Society had attended a meeting only a few days before, when Edith Gittins and Mrs Ramsay MacDonald and her daughter attended a non-militant meeting in Exeter Hall. Margaret MacDonald later said of her daughter attending the NUWSS meeting, 'I hope she will thank me when she grows up for being so considerate. I hope she will be proud of it.' Although this was basically a non-militant meeting, it demonstrates the early co-operation between the different groups as the WSPU were courteously invited. As Sylvia Pankhurst later recalled:

'A crowd of the non-militants assembled close to the Achilles Statue at Hyde Park Corner. It was a dismal wet Saturday afternoon, but in spite of the rain and the muddy streets a procession of women half a mile in length was formed and marched steadily on to attend the meeting in Exeter Hall in the Strand and Trafalgar Square. The procession was afterwards known as the "Mud March".'

By now, most women attending these meetings fully understood that should there be no mention of female suffrage in the King's Speech, then there would be a full assault on Parliament with the risk of arrest and imprisonment, and by the afternoon of Wednesday 13 February 1907 it had become clear to those waiting in Caxton Hall that no mention of female suffrage had been made.

Incensed by what she deemed as the Government's lack of commitment to this issue, Mrs Pankhurst rallied those present to march on Parliament and demand an audience with the Prime Minister. Over 300 women, led by Mrs Despard, marched the short distance to the House of Commons where they were met by a cordon of policemen along the perimeters of Abbey Green. Undaunted by the odds, the women engaged the police in a struggle that was to drag on into the early evening. At one point, Alice Hawkins later recalled, mounted police appeared and, 'taking the place of Cossacks', rode the women down. Later, Alice Hawkins wrote to Ramsay MacDonald from Holloway Prison and asked him to object in the strongest terms to the Home Secretary for 'ordering mounted police out to ride down women…no other civilised country would treat women in such a manner'.

Suffragettes being arrested outside the House of Commons in 1907.

Along with Alice Hawkins, over 50 women were arrested, including two other Leicester women, Miss Knight and Miss Wells. *The Pioneer's* report at the time stated that when they were released on bail, they returned to Caxton Hall to recover their wits and prepare themselves for a second attack. However, during the ensuing fight 11 members did manage to reach the Members' Lobby, only to be ejected later.

The decision to go to prison was no small matter to the Leicester women and not done lightly. Their position was not of 'rebels' but of thoughtful women, ready to risk all in the struggle to win the vote. And although Alice Hawkins was not yet a member of the WSPU, prison had a profound effect on her; much of what she saw both horrified and alarmed her. This experience intensified her belief in women's rights and convinced her to form a branch of the WSPU in Leicester. From her prison notes it is possible to see this commitment grow, as she recalled with some gloom the down-trodden women in Holloway:

'One in particular that I saw in church set me thinking whatever could have brought her to prison. She was a girl not more than 16 with oh, such a sweet face and pathetic eyes. I could not keep my eyes off her every time we went to church…many's the time my heart ached for the poor women that are in for hard labour, for it is one long grind from early morning until late at night.'

Unfortunately, the publicity surrounding the assault on Parliament did little back in Leicester to cement the growing tensions between the militant and non-militant groups. Although there is little evidence available to gauge the extent to which this difference of opinion went, it is clear from isolated reports in local newspapers that a rift was certainly appearing, and, almost from the start, local, middle-class women of influence like Edith Gittins, Fanny Fullager, Charlotte and Isobel Ellis, Miss Von Petzold of the National Union of Women's Suffrage Society and Mrs Ramsay MacDonald of the Women's Labour League declined any association with the WSPU branch, and apologised in a letter for their non-attendance at the first meeting. Entirely reflecting the 'respectable' view of the suffragist, they believed the actions of the WSPU were beyond the pale and dangerous. Indeed, this difference of attitude towards the methods employed by the different factions was clearly spelt out by Edith Gittins of the Leicester branch of the NUWSS in April 1907, when she addressed a meeting of the WLL.

In this speech she admitted that opinions greatly differed between the two organisations and argued that the WSPU were not only putting the clock back in the female suffrage, but it was also connecting 'women with feeble violence and hysteria'. Ironically, rather than embracing Christabel's desire to have women of influence and position join the movement, the actions of February 1907 had precisely the opposite effect in Leicester as many working-class women within the boot and shoe industry flocked to join. However, not all middle-class women were given to Edith Gittins's point of view, and later, as the WSPU grew in influence and prestige towards the end of 1909, some younger women would turn their back on the NUWSS and join the WSPU.

In other ways, too, the actions of the women in London alienated other organisations that could well have been natural allies. For instance, the actions of Alice Hawkins, Mrs Catlin, Miss Wells and Miss Knight appalled and horrified the new ILP member for Leicester, James Ramsay MacDonald, and although he was by and large in favour of enfranchising women, he strongly rejected any method that was neither democratic nor peaceful. Interestingly enough, whereas others within the WSPU criticised the leadership for being undemocratic within the organisation, MacDonald

Alice Hawkins's police charge sheet. She kept this in her scrapbook.

No. 114.

METROPOLITAN POLICE.

_a_ Division.

Cannon Row Station.

Take Notice, that you _Mrs Alice Hawkins_

are bound in the sum of _Two Pounds_ Pounds to

appear at the _Westminster_ Police Court, situated at

Rochester Row at _10_

o'clock _A_ M., on the _14th_ day of _Feby_

190 _7_, to answer the charge of * _Disorderly Conduct_
& resisting Police

and unless you then appear there, further proceedings will be taken.

Dated this _13th_ day of _Feby_

One Thousand Nine Hundred _7_

R. Fisher

Officer on Duty.

* Being found drunk in a public street, or being guilty, while drunk, of disorderly behaviour in a street,
or whatever the charge may be.

25000 | 4 | 06. M.P. [201].

Votes for Women.

RELEASED SUFFRAGISTS.

LABOUR PARTY SECRETARY'S CRITICISM.

The prisoners in Holloway Jail were awakened yesterday morning by the joyful strains of the London Excelsior Band, which had come to serenade the twenty-nine suffragists whose fourteen days' imprisonment in connexion with the recent demonstration outside the House of Commons had expired.

For more than an hour the band played the stirring marching songs of the Women's Social and Political Union, the leading members of which had also gathered outside under their banners. Cheer upon cheer greeted the appearance of Miss Christabel Pankhurst, LL.B., and her twenty-eight comrades, whose names are as follows: Mrs. Armitage, Bradford; Miss F. Bright, London; Miss Cairns, Glasgow; Mrs. Drysdale, London; Miss FitzHerbert, Battersea, London; Mrs. Fielding, Bradford; Mrs. Hawkins, Leicester; Mrs. Holmes, Croydon; Miss Holland, Manchester; Miss Nellie Kenney, Bradford; Miss King, Bradford; Mrs. Moffatt, Glasgow; Miss Harriet Rozier, London; Mrs. Rigby, Preston; Mrs. Roy Rothwell, Battersea, London; Miss Elsie Stephenson, Leeds; Mrs. Sproson, Wolverhampton; Mrs. Stephenson, Leeds; Miss Seruya, Chelsea, S.W.; Miss Ellen Smith, Croydon; Miss Wolff von Sandau, London; Miss Mary Smith, Manchester; Mrs. Sanders, Battersea; Miss Margaret Smith, Chelsea; Mrs. Taylor, Hedben Bridge; Miss Varley, Bradford; Mrs. Whitworth, Sheffield; and Mrs. Yates, Sheffield.

Still accompanied by the band, and with flying banners, the suffragists proceeded to Caledonian-road Station. Great enthusiasm marked the progress of this early morning procession, which, after leaving the Holborn Tube station, marched via Kingsway and the Strand to the Eustace Miles Restaurant, where a "reformed" breakfast awaited them.

AT THE BREAKFAST.

Mr. H. W. Nevinson, the war correspondent, presided at the breakfast, and among those who were present to welcome the prisoners were Mrs. Pankhurst, Mrs. Cobden Unwin, Mrs. Cobden-Sanderson, Mr. and Mrs. Pethick Lawrence, Miss Elizabeth Robins, and Mrs. Morgan Richards. Mr. and Mrs. Bernard Shaw, Mr. and Mrs. Zangwill, and several M.P.s wrote regretting their inability to be present.

Two very interesting letters had been received by Mrs. Pethick Lawrence, one enclosing a cheque for £57, being a contribution of £1 to the funds of the union for each of the fifty-seven women who had gone to prison. The second letter is an interesting indication of the line of action being taken by many women, who are refusing to pay their Income tax.

In moving a resolution of thanks to the suffragist ex-prisoners for the services they had rendered to the cause, Mr. Nevinson expressed approval and admiration both of their aims and of their methods.

Alderman Sanders, L.C.C., the husband of one of the released ladies, seconded.

Miss Christabel Pankhurst, who on rising received quite an ovation from the two hundred odd guests, spoke of the recent disturbance as the twentieth century Peterloo. She predicted trouble in the constituencies of those members who were down to move the rejection of Mr. Dickinson's Women's Enfranchisement Bill. "If they kill this Bill," she added, "politics will change. If we do not get the vote it will mean revolution amongst women."

Many of the other ex-prisoners gave their experiences of Holloway, all of them declaring their readiness to return there if necessary.

Miss Florence Bright, a well-known novelist, and the first of her calling to go to jail for the suffrage, explained that, though connected with the other societies, she was not a member of the union, and had been arrested merely because, knowing something about horses, she had tried to stop the horse of one of the mounted policemen.

THE I.L.P.'S ATTITUDE.

The sensation of the day, however, was provided by Mrs. Hawkins, of Leicester, who read the following letter which had been addressed to her in Holloway by "A Member of Parliament who promised to vote for a Women's Suffrage Bill."

"Dear Mrs. Hawkins,—I got your letter from the Westminster Police Court, and was sorry to find that you had been run in. I really do not think you are doing any good to the cause. Up to a certain point the action of the W.S. and P.U. was excellent. It stirred up public interest in the question, and would no doubt have secured that some Women's Enfranchisement Bill would have been passed this Parliament. Now I am afraid you have lost all chance of that.

"The Belfast resolution was carried owing to the foolish antics of those women who went to Cockermouth and Huddersfield, and there will be a much bigger vote against women's enfranchisement at the I.L.P. Conference this year than ever there has been before."

Pressed for the name of the writer, Mrs. Hawkins stated that the letter was from Mr. J. Ramsay MacDonald, M.P., secretary of the Labour Party.

Experiences in Gaol.

To a Press representative Miss E. Gillett, of Cardiff, said: "I didn't mind going to Holloway at all, but the only thing that pained me was being shut in between four walls. I had plenty of clothes to wear, but they were very non-hygienic and uncomfortable. It was a green dress, and simply smothered with the broad arrow, but a number of people would be only too glad to wear it. The wardresses, with a few exceptions, were very kind. One, however, on the first night I was placed in my cell brought my supper, and instead of handing it to me in a ladylike manner she flung it on the table. When we arrived at the prison we all had to take off our clothes and indulge in a bath. There were three wardresses in the room, and they spoke in a gruff and assertive manner, but, of course, there was no need for them to be so emphatic.

"I went to chapel every day. The chaplain wished me every happiness, but he appeared to be rather a meek man, and I think he was afraid of us. On Sunday he preached against the sin of cheap popularity, and he hinted it would be well if we didn't grumble against present-day conditions."

A page of newspaper clippings from Alice's scrapbook.

attacked the WSPU for being undemocratic within the political system itself. The classic dilemma faced by any militant organisation is whether they become more moderate to gain acceptance within Parliament or retain their militant policies and be met with scepticism and hostility.

By doing the latter, MacDonald believed the WSPU, by association, would bring into disrepute all other suffrage organisations and make them less effective. But, more importantly, he argued that the WSPU was an elitist organisation that only sought to promote the interests of a small number of middle-class women, thereby being unrepresentative of all women. In a letter to Alice Hawkins he complained that little good would come of such actions and warned her that any use of violence would completely alienate the Labour movement from the WSPU. As he wrote:

> 'I really do not think you are doing any good to the cause. Up to a certain point the action of the WS and Pu [sic] was excellent. It stirred up public interest in the question, and would no doubt have secured that some Women's Enfranchisement Bill would have been passed this Parliament. Now I am afraid you have lost all chance of that. The Belfast resolution was carried owing to the foolish antics of those women who went to Cockermouth and Huddersfield, and there will be a much bigger vote against women's enfranchisement at the ILP Conference this coming year.'

Opposite: Newspaper clipping from Alice Hawkins's scrapbook which mention her arrest and dramatic reading of Ramsay MacDonald's letter.

Notwithstanding, this reply came as something of a surprise to Alice Hawkins languishing in Holloway prison. It appears she had expected far greater support from MacDonald and regretted his reticence to get involved. Neither was she in any mood for compromise or, indeed, a retreat from the militant path she had now chosen. She was adamant that she was doing the right thing and argued that she was prepared to reject the Labour Party in favour of the WSPU if it continued to fail the women and their cause. All working people had 'to suffer for every reform', she wrote in a caustic letter back to Ramsay MacDonald, and made her position more than clear when she added:

A dashing young Ramsay MacDonald. This picture was found in Alice Hawkins's scrapbook.

'I was sorry to see the stand you take over the enfranchisement of women, for I quite thought you were in favour of it, but I see I was mistaken. Now as to the ILP voting against the enfranchisement of women [the Belfast Resolution] I hope not!! For if they do, I am afraid they will lose a great deal number of members. And just now I would think they are quite afraid to do that, as I understand the equality of the sexes is one of their chief items in it [the ILP programme].'

However, to understand MacDonald's position, an awareness of his politics is much needed. In essence, MacDonald was a reserved, aloof and obstinate man who owed more to his lowly Scottish background than he did to his political convictions, and as such came to advocate a slow and cautious approach that could only be termed as 'socialism by instalments'. This was all the more important in that it signalled a change of thought and direction within socialist circles. No longer was socialism to be an ideology of revolution, whereby power was achieved outside of government. Instead, it was destined to become, under the 'Lossie Loon', a blueprint of change by evolutionary means. As MacDonald himself pointed out in *Socialism And Society*:

'The scheme upon which humanity evolves to higher and more humane stages of existence is either rational or it is not. If it is not, all organised attempts to hasten reform and make it effective…are wasted efforts.'

It is here in this passage that the kernel of Ramsay MacDonald's political philosophy can be found. He had been a socialist since his youth in Lossiemouth, where he read Henry George's *Progress and Poverty* in 1881. It was from this book, according to MacDonald's biographer Hessell Tiltman, that MacDonald became familiar with the idea of common ownership of property and the principle of a greater share in the aggregate wealth of the nation. But, more importantly, it galvanised MacDonald's thinking and allowed him, with the help of Keir Hardie, to develop a new breed of socialist thought that would drive a wedge between the old continental revolutionary socialism and the milder, democratic British socialism that was more suited to this country. Yet, ironically, this type of thinking was very similar to Edmund Burke's conservatism and

Alices's reply to Ramsay MacDonald's letter was preserved in her scrapbook.

alluded to the analogy of society as a social organism, and that the life of the organism is conducted through change. And, like Burke, he flinched from any social movement that directly attacked the status quo without regard to tradition and an evolutionary path to the past.

Consequently, when the militant campaign began in 1903, he lambasted its methods as being without the light of reason or morals. Instead, he argued that if women were to get the vote, then it must be done through the organisation of opinion and the operation of a constructive genius. The injustices found within society have to be resolved by what he thought of as organic changes of a progressive nature. Social and political change was a scientific progress rather than a violent upheaval of popular revolt, however justified. It was not that MacDonald lacked the qualities to see the validity of the WSPU's arguments, especially when linked to the degrading poverty encountered by many working women, but that the actions advocated by Mrs Pankhurst and her followers balked against everything he believed in. Violent protest and party disunity could only do more harm than good. Any changes to the franchise had to come from the whole of society, and not from any marginal section.

To do otherwise would jeopardise and endanger the organic unity. Evolution, not revolution, was the way forward. It was about maintaining an organic wholeness and a moral growth based on a social intellect. It could never be about social divisions and class struggles; that was the doctrine and dogma of the European Marxist. In Britain it was the pursuit of moderate respectability and the need to work within the existing framework that was more important. Consequently, the WSPU and their reactionary methods would only divide the different suffrage groups. This line of thinking was outlined by Ramsay MacDonald in a speech in 1908 at the Free Christian Church in Leicester. Instead of promoting the actions of the WSPU as vital to the struggle, he highlighted the problems as he saw them when he said:

'We are quite aware of the enthusiasm of the WSPU and of the quieter, more dignified work of the WSS. But they have not to convince men so much as their own sisters…as soon as the whole body of women ask for the vote they will unquestionably get it.'

This was, of course, a classic clash between the very distinct traditional characteristics of British socialism, which epitomised the bitter debate raging within the ranks of the Left. On the one hand, MacDonald espoused caution and patience, while, on the other, Alice Hawkins was seeking to destroy a competitive system through the use of syndicalism, tempered with the Social Democratic Federation's Marxist philosophy of insurrection. She believed, along with other militant Labour leaders like Tom Mann, Will Thorne and Ben Tillett, that the new unions, to which women were now joining in large numbers, were destined to become the main democratic organisations of the future. They, not private capital, would own the industries their members worked in, like the small co-operative factories that were already springing up, and, ultimately, they would control the country's economic and social policies. Yet, despite these grand designs, the importance of the co-operative ideal in forming socialist principles should not be overlooked in the Leicester experience, as other historians, notably Bill Lancaster, have noted:

'The co-operative ideal had such potency that it had become central to the socialist platform and touched a nerve that ran to the heart of young socialist trade unionists during the early 1890s.'

But all this would be achieved, not by political action in terms of forced legislation, but by direct action outside of Parliament, inside the world of economics. There is, of course, a paradox here that fits uneasily within the context of what has been said, in that Alice Hawkins, although a syndicalist, still argued that the vote was important to women in order that they might be able to change their condition through Government intervention. Further, there is much difficulty in trying to trace a link with the influence of European Marxist ideology on trade union members in order to justify a revolutionary conspiracy, but Hyndman's Social Democratic Federation was a successful training school for a succession of the most gifted working-class militants like Tom Mann and Will Thorne. Moreover, Alice Hawkins had often made it clear that she was a follower of Tom Mann, and even linked her incarceration in Holloway in 1907 to his campaigns and earlier imprisonment for trade union militancy.

It might well be argued that Ramsay MacDonald was, in reality, only following the party line after Christabel's attack on the ILP candidates at the Cockermouth and Huddersfield by-elections in 1906, yet throughout the period MacDonald, if nothing else, was totally consistent in his approach to the WSPU. This was aptly demonstrated at the ILP's conference in Derby in 1907; after the delegates sent Mrs Pankhurst a letter of support, he sarcastically retaliated in the *Labour Leader* that he 'regretted the decision' and he thought that the 'special applause of the women who have gone to prison on this occasion is false sentiment'. He went on to argue that:

'The resolution was carried because the delegates were full of generous thoughts...There is more of the Christmas spirit of charity in our ILP conference than any gathering that has ever met since the little gathering in the upper room of Jerusalem.'

He complained, with some justification, that the WSPU only focused on one area of social inequality. Yet, while this might well have been true of the leadership in London, the evidence of the Leicester suffragettes suggested that they still regarded themselves as an integral part of the Labour movement and attempted to focus on many different aspects of social inequality faced by women. It is, however, important to note that for Alice Hawkins the lack of political enfranchisement was the root of all women's problems. And while this might well have been a simplistic view, it was, nevertheless, a motivating factor that cannot be readily overlooked and explains much of their outlook and later actions. Moreover, the existing evidence also suggests that Leicester was not alone in this respect. As Sylvia Pankhurst pointed out, in May 1906 the Glasgow branch of the union attempted to interview the President of the Local Government Board of Trade on behalf of the unemployed, finally sending him a resolution supporting the demand of the Labour Party that unemployment should take precedence over all other questions during the session of Parliament.

If this was true, then clearly a reassessment of MacDonald's early antagonism towards the suffragette movement is surely needed. It has been argued that his hostility to the WSPU indicated a degree of jealousy concerning the impact the suffragette campaign was having on women within the Labour movement. This view is not as far-fetched as it might seem, in that both Keir Hardie and Sylvia Pankhurst later claimed that the Women's Labour League was formed by Mrs Margaret MacDonald and, ironically, Alice Hawkins, at the behest of Ramsay MacDonald, in 1906 to help stem the flow of women out of the socialist and Labour movement.

Indeed, Keir Hardie vehemently opposed the formation of the WLL on the grounds that he saw the organisation as a dangerous rival to the WSPU. It may be reasonable to assume, of course, that his relationship with Sylvia Pankhurst had much to do with this stance. Yet in one so complex, this could never be the only reason, and it is important to remember, therefore, that during the early years of feminist militancy Keir Hardie still regarded the WSPU as part of the Labour movement and to this end believed they warranted all due support. Interestingly enough, this position was not shared by some of the Leicester women, as Alice Hawkins, one of the founder members of the Leicester branch, also helped form the local WLL with Margaret MacDonald.

On returning to Leicester, Alice Hawkins, with the support of her husband Alfred, continued to work towards the formation of a branch of the WSPU in Leicester. As it has already been pointed out, her experiences with the Pankhursts in gaol had a profound impression on her life and on her return to the town she set about realising her goal. With the help of her friend and fellow-social campaigner the Revd F.L. Donaldson, they organised a meeting, again in the Boot and Shoe Trade Hall, for WSPU members to come and talk about their experiences of prison life.

This time, however, Alice Hawkins shared the platform with three WSPU veterans of the assault on Parliament: Mary Gawthorpe, Mrs Rothwell and Christabel Pankhurst. Thus, it was with the help of a national leader, Mary Gawthorpe, that Alice Hawkins was able to form the Leicester branch of the WSPU during March 1907.

Mary Gawthorpe.

In many ways Mary Gawthorpe was the natural choice to help start and organise the Leicester women. She was a working woman who had joined the suffrage movement by way of socialism and Labour politics. In Leeds, as Alice Hawkins had done in Leicester, she had helped form a local branch of the Women's Labour League and had quickly become an executive committee member, meeting many leaders of the women's trade union movement, including Mary Macarthur and Gertrude Tuckwell. Again, in much the same way as Alice Hawkins, she believed that the WSPU was dominated by socialist suffragists, although 'the national leadership was undoubtedly more determined on a separation from its socialist origins than many of its members'.

However, in the early summer of 1907 the campaign was so successful that Alice Hawkins was

Mary Macarthur.

able to state by 21 March that a Leicester branch of the WSPU had been set up and that the first full meeting of the branch would take place on 9 April 1907 at the Welford Coffee House, with Mrs Barnes of Harrow Road presiding.

The choice of venue is in itself an interesting one and probably reflects the temperance influence that was brought to the movement by women like Mrs Carryer, a Poor Law Guardian, and the Reverend Donaldson's wife. Coffee house meetings at the turn of the century were part and parcel of Victorian life in Leicester. As E. Hepple Hall pointed out in his study of coffee houses in Leicester, *Coffee Taverns, Cocoa Houses And Coffee Palaces,* the Temperance Movement clearly saw the need for places where the working man could meet, talk and play games away from the public house. However, according to *Spencer's Guide,* the excellent refreshments found within coffee houses tended to make them more popular with the more affluent middle-class rather than the class for whom they were primarily established.

Yet Leicester was not unique in this connection between suffrage societies and coffee houses. In Newcastle, for example, socialists and suffrage groups also used similar venues. For example, the Blackett Street/Northumberland Street area was home to a number of small cafés, which were the meeting places for radicals and early socialists. One of those cafés – the *Drawing Room Café* – became the meeting place for the North Eastern Society for Women's Suffrage.

In Leicester, from notes taken at the meeting it is known that letters of apology for non-attendance were read by Miss Evelyn Carryer from Lady Rolleston and Mrs Margaret MacDonald. For her part, Margaret MacDonald saw nothing but disaster as a result of militancy. All her sentiments were against what the WSPU later stood for. As she said at the time, she felt far more injured than the brawlers were hurt themselves, and, tackling Alice Hawkins head on, she scorned the idea that there was anything in common between the WSPU's militancy and revolution.

Although these women had refused to join because of the growing militancy, others undoubtedly did join, and it is interesting to note that not only were the ILP and the Liberal Party represented, but also a selection of working women from the Women's Conservative Association were also present. In a stirring speech to the new converts, Mrs Emmeline Pankhurst claimed that the success of the union was due to the earnestness of purpose and self-sacrifice of individuality which actuated every member.

Thus, almost despite the early differences of opinion between the militant and non-militant factions, the claim by the Leicester WSPU that they had broken down all political barriers appeared true. In reality, however, the formation of the Leicester branch of the WSPU represented a very fragile amalgamation of working and middle-class women which would later collapse under the weight of militancy.

By all accounts, the first meeting was something of a success, and not only had they placed womanhood before party politics, but they also enrolled 30 new members for the organisation. Unfortunately, their baptism of fire into the WSPU proved a costly affair for some of the Leicester delegates at Caxton Hall in February, as the minutes of the second Leicester WSPU meeting demonstrated. At this meeting letters of reply were read from local MPs rejecting a request that they should interest themselves on behalf of the Leicester girls (sadly unnamed) who were dismissed from their employment for 'leaving their place of work without intimating where they were going'.

Almost from the beginning, the infant branch of the WSPU blossomed under the guidance of national leaders coming to Leicester over the summer months, not only to speak at open-air meetings in the marketplace and the Corn Exchange, but also to organise and instruct the local branch in the importance of 'At Homes'. These gatherings were started by the Pankhursts and were

Christabel Pankhurst in Trafalgar Square, encouraging women to 'rush the House of Commons'.

Suffragettes dressed in prison uniforms.

of immense value in clarifying WSPU strategy and monitoring the political situation both at national and local level. All organisers were encouraged to attend 'At Homes', and Mrs Pethick-Lawrence advocated that the members should read at least two newspapers with differing political views each day.

Of course, that does not mean to say that the importance of open-air meetings was not appreciated by local and national figures. Alice Hawkins and other working-class radicals, like Bertha Clark and the trade unionist Lizzie Willson, understood only too well the importance of such events and concentrated their energies on them in order to get their message across. Indeed, as Christabel Pankhurst told her followers in the spring of 1909:

> 'In all parts of the country during the summer they will be holding open-air meetings in parks, at street corners and at factory gates, for this is the best of all means at polarising a movement.'

It is important to stress here the importance of such gatherings in an age before mass information technology, like radio and television. Yet, in Leicester the first big meeting on 6 June 1907 proved to be something of a flop when bad weather prevented Miss Gawthorpe, the guest speaker from Clement's Inn, from delivering her message. Still undeterred, many more meetings were conducted, with, perhaps, the most successful occurring during July when both Alice Hawkins and Sylvia Pankhurst addressed what was deemed to be at the time a 'huge crowd in the marketplace'.

Both Sylvia Pankhurst and Mary Gawthorpe had been in and around Leicestershire since 11 June, when they had completed a successful campaign in the Rutland by-election against the Liberal candidate W.F. Lyon in Oakham. It is not clear to what extent the local WSPU played a part in this campaign, but during May a combined deputation of local WSPU members and the NUWSS arrived to see Evan Barlow, Lyon's election agent in Oakham. At this meeting, both Evelyn Carryer of the WSPU and Miss Palliseer, parliamentary secretary for the NUWSS, pledged to render all assistance if he would openly support women's suffrage. However, no pledge was received, and both the WSPU and the NUWSS energetically went into opposition to make it a three-cornered fight. Although their political strategy differed and their election policies frequently conflicted, there were numerous instances of co-operation between the two wings of the movement during the early years of militancy. However, as the WSPU broke new ground in their fight for the vote, the different movements drifted even further apart.

After the election, Christabel Pankhurst claimed the tactics of the WSPU allowed the Conservative candidate to almost double his majority, but really there is no serious way of assessing the real influence of the WSPU at these by-elections. There was, however, a real attempt on behalf of the union to make life difficult for any returning Government MPs. This strategy entirely reflected the policy instigated by Christabel to put the WSPU on the political map. Indeed, Christabel made this point quite clear and argued that any denial of the WSPU's existence and importance amounted to self-delusion, 'But this, like other illusions, will disappear as they find it more and more impossible to get elected to the House of Commons.'

In some ways, however, Sylvia Pankhurst differed from the other members of her family in that she sought not only to mobilise middle-class women, but also whole sections of the women's labour movement. As a committed socialist, she naturally saw the benefits of organising women both in and out of the trade union movement. Thus, she was instinctively drawn to the working-class women who were to make up the sum of the WSPU in Leicester. It was here that she began to formulate her ideas of working with working-class women, which would materialise some years later when she would go and work among the working-class women in the East End of London. In her later book, *The Suffragette Movement. An Intimate Account Of Persons And Ideals,* she recalled the start of the WSPU in Leicester and the beginning of her long campaign to try and establish

Modern reconstructions of Sylvia Pankhurst's picture inside the Equity today.

Opposite: This picture, drawn by Sylvia Pankhurst, has recently been purchased by the museum service in Leicester.

Working women in the Equity, the cradle of the suffragette movement in Leicester, drawn by Sylvia Pankhurst during her stay in 1907.

and expand an industrial base for the WSPU with working women. As she wrote:

'I moved to Leicester to work among the women in the shoemaking industry. Mrs Hawkins, the WSPU secretary, was also active in the Bootmaker's Union. She introduced me to a small producer's co-operative factory [The Equity Co-operative boot and shoe factory]... At night I held meetings for the local WSPU, amongst whom only Mrs Hawkins, as yet, dared mount the platform. The members were then almost all working class. One of them was a collector of laundry accounts, struggling to support a younger sister and brother. She had published a first novel and was casually employed by a local newspaper which obligingly permitted her to give good reports of our work.'[4]

During Sylvia's summer sojourn in Leicester, her stay was cut short by a telegram from Christabel recalling her back to London to support the family against what she saw as a damaging rift between Mrs Billington-Greig and herself. In spite of every effort on the part of Mrs Pankhurst to maintain a show of unity, destructive criticisms of their methods and leadership led to the charge that the organisation was undemocratic. To some extent, this observation was more than true as it had become clear to the Pankhursts that it would be impossible to run the union on a representational basis and, as a result, just a month before the national conference Mrs Pankhurst tore up the WSPU's constitution and announced that a new committee was to be selected.[5] As a result, the WSPU came under the control of Mrs Pankhurst, and local WSPU groups would be subjected to direction from Clement's Inn.

For many sections within the organisation, this centralisation of WSPU policy proved to be too bitter a pill to swallow, and Mrs Despard, the leader of several assaults on Parliament, and Teresa Billington-Greig resigned their membership and formed The Women's Freedom League. As a result, the latter part of 1907 was to be something of a turning point in the outlook of the WSPU, both nationally and locally. As the organisation grew and became more militant, around the country splits began to appear that would ultimately cleave off something in the region of 20 percent of the membership. These rifts were more or less a direct result of the early success the WSPU achieved. Indeed, by the end of 1907 there were already over 70 branches nationwide. In fact, the movement had become so popular that many of the old-established suffrage societies had joined the militants while still clinging to the idea of a democratic organisation.

As elsewhere, this schism was potentially damaging to the continuation of the WSPU in Leicester, as the debate now focused around the need for democratic input into the movement, and several women declared that they would not tolerate what Ramsay MacDonald would later call that 'evil junta'. But, despite a few dissenting voices, notably Mrs Catlin (wife of a local councillor) and later in the year Miss Carryer, the split seemed to have had little effect on the movement locally, and as early as June 1907 the Leicester WSPU agreed at a meeting to participate in the forthcoming testimonials to be presented to Mrs Billington-Greig.

For her part, Miss Carryer appeared to have become increasingly concerned, both at the lack of democratic procedures within the organisation and the increasing level of militant action. Consequently, by May 1908 she had, to all intents and purposes, broken her links with the WSPU and moved over to the more democratic and less militant NUWSS. However, despite her disquiet at the methods of control employed by the Pankhursts, the tactics of the militants very much appealed to her radicalism as she continued to subscribe financially to the WSPU through to 1914. Moreover, she occasionally joined WSPU meetings when famous celebrities came to town.

Paradoxically, her desertion occurred almost in spite of an emotive appeal by Mrs Pethick-Lawrence to hold the movement together. She had arrived in the town at the request of Mrs Carryer to speak at a meeting in the Welford Coffee House and attempted to rally the troops around the new leadership. She argued that the measures taken by Mrs Pankhurst were right and claimed that the militant actions the WSPU had taken over the previous two years had brought the whole issue of women's suffrage to the fore. As she explained, 'the WSPU had made a moribund thing and live a burning question'.

In the end, Mrs Pethick-Lawrence had little to fear in the way of a mass desertion from the Leicester branch. The majority of working women who made up the active membership stayed loyal to the Pankhursts. Alice Hawkins and Bertha Clark, both strong trade union members, not only appeared to submerge their loyalties to the ILP but also to the Labour movement in general by accepting the

Pankhursts' dictum that all members could not belong to another political organisation while they were in the WSPU. This complete acceptance of WSPU policy was later demonstrated in October 1907 when, because of a quirk in the Franchise Act, some women were allowed not only to vote, but also to stand as local councillors. This was too good a chance to miss and the WSPU actively supported Evelyn Carryer as an 'independent' against Harry Woolley, the Labour candidate in the Wycliffe Ward. Needless to say, the WSPU failed to attract enough support to allow Evelyn Carryer to win, possibly because not all women had the vote nor could they claim to be a major political party speaking for working-class concerns. However, it was a step in the right direction and complied with WSPU policy to make political life difficult for all parties.

The group were at this time, regardless of the initial mix between the social classes, a living example of what Bernard Shaw believed women should be, namely a trade unionist, a suffragette and, last but not least, a socialist. Without doubt, Alice Hawkins and some of her colleagues, like Evelyn Close, Bertha Clark and Mrs Barnes, were already all three, and while national issues and policies were being taken in London, the Leicester branch undertook to do what they could do best – to fight for the interests of working women.

All in all, the first year of the Leicester WSPU had been something of a success. The movement had survived its first split and, mainly through the efforts of Alice Hawkins and Bertha Clark, the union had managed to recruit a substantial number of dissatisfied women from the Boot and Shoe industry. Subsequently, Alice Hawkins felt justifiably confident to proclaim that she spoke for the majority of working women when she sent her telegram to Asquith in December 1907 saying:

A newspaper cutting from Alice Hawkins's scrapbook.

THREE MORE SUFFRAGETTES RELEASED FROM HOLLOWAY GAOL YESTERDAY.

Mr and Mrs Pethick-Lawrence with Christabel Pankhurst.

'Is there any possible chance of votes for women being included in the King's Speech? Kindly reply… A hundred thousand Leicester women await your answer.'

As might be expected, the Prime Minister declined to answer and Alice Hawkins's plea went unheard. However, the resolve of the Leicester women was as strong as ever, and over the following years it would stand the test of time.

The formation of the branch in 1907 clearly shows that they were quite different from other groups around the East Midlands and, as a result, their interests were directed at the conscious political attitudes of not only themselves, but also those of the local ILP. However, as the Pankhursts increased their grip on the union as a whole, much of this was to change.

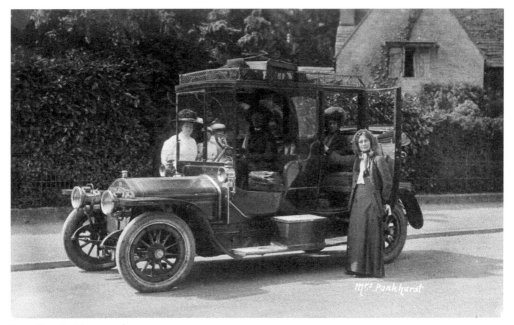

Emmeline Pankhurst and the official WSPU motor car.

Yet they still believed that they could do something to improve their lot, or more importantly the lot of working women. This was not only fundamental to the individual's political beliefs, but also to their attitude towards authority. They were, in the main, more willing to take risks and were unconcerned about the social stigma that went with going to gaol. Of course, many middle-class women also went to gaol, but the economic and social restrictions on these women were far greater.

In general, it was because of their social and economic background that their motivations were undoubtedly different. This was reflected, to a larger degree, in their social outlook and corresponds with an almost left-wing philosophical view that demanded political freedom for oneself and for all women, although this condition was later overturned when it was decreed by the Pankhursts that the fight for the vote should only focus on middle-class women, a stance that ultimately led to the withdrawal of Labour support in Leicester. Nevertheless, at first the intentions were clearly there, expressed in the sentiments of one local suffragette who believed in a freedom which allowed the individual to make her own happiness and develop the principle of equality without being in opposition to others.

Indeed, this freedom would only be possible if it was developed on the basis of solidarity with other women from different social backgrounds. Political doctrines cover not only a number of attitudes, but also appeal to specific emotions and passions, and on this note the Pankhursts were more than able to channel the dissatisfaction many women felt at the time, but it was to a specific end that had little to do with solidarity. What damage the Pankhursts did when they divorced themselves from the working class is hard to say, but it undoubtedly had a major effect on the way in which the WSPU was to later develop.

Notes

1   Mrs Cobden-Saunderson was the daughter of the Liberal radical Richard Cobden.
2   Mrs Edith Barnes was at this time Honorary Secretary to the Women's Labour League.
3   They travelled down on the Tuesday and stayed with Mrs Quilter and Mr Neal, who was then the editor of *The Sentinel. The Pioneer*, 16 February 1907.
4   This woman called herself Lydia and had been writing a women's column for *The Pioneer* since 1902.
5   The national WSPU was under the control of Emmeline and Christabel Pankhurst, who were now to be responsible for the entire organisation. From this point on, it was decided that there would be no membership fee, only the signing of this pledge, 'I endorse the objects and methods of the WSPU, and I hereby undertake not to support the candidate of any political party at Parliamentary elections until women have obtained the Parliamentary vote.'

UNDAUNTED!

Photo. by " Daily Mirror."

THE ARREST OF
MISS GRACE ROE.

A postcard of Grace Roe's arrest from Alice Hawkins's scrapbook.

Chapter Three
Growth of the Pankhurst Autocracy and its Consequences

'You think with your gloved hands you can cure the trouble
of the century.'
John Galsworthy, *Strife*

As 1908 dawned with its high hopes and optimism, it was to be something of an *annus mirabilis* for the WSPU in Leicester. At the beginning of the year the branch was in place and ready to face the coming fight. However, the strengths and weaknesses of the branch were about to be thrown into sharp relief by factors that were outside their control. In Clement's Inn a shift of focus had taken place that can now be seen as an independent variable in the process of change that was to sweep across the provincial branches from 1908 onwards. For example, not only did the Leicester women appear to move away from their Labour roots towards a more feminist, militant position, but the branch also slowly began to change in social composition with the enrolment of a selection of middle-class women.

Of course, it can be argued that these two factors were inexorably linked, that indeed the influx of younger and more militant middle-class women would inevitably change the branch, but this metamorphosis was not a local phenomenon and had its roots elsewhere. Certainly it can be traced back to the directions and instructions given out by the leadership in London. On 30 May in the Exeter Hall, Mrs Pethick-Lawrence told the audience 'If you have an influential position, socially or professionally, we want you!' Some years later Christabel Pankhurst put it more firmly when she wrote the working-women's movement was of no value: their lives were too hard, their education too meagre to equip them for the struggle.

Instead, the fight was to be controlled and conducted by women who had 'drawn prizes in the lucky bag of life'. On these points, however, it is important to bear in mind that any policies introduced by the Pankhursts and the Pethick-Lawrences in London would, by their very nature, have a direct influence on the membership in

Opposite: Miss Christabel Pankhurst.

Leicester. The WSPU was not, by any stretch of the imagination, a democratic organisation where members could vote on or trading implement policy issues. Instead, when directives and policies were instigated by Clement's Inn the branches were expected to follow them without question. Indeed, to do otherwise meant that members ran the risk of expulsion.

In order to understand this crucial shift and the motives behind the Pankhursts' desire to control the WSPU at a regional level, it is necessary to appreciate the concerns and anxieties within the personality of Christabel Pankhurst. She, more than anyone else, was responsible for the way in which the branches would grow, and her insistence on recruiting middle-class women into the organisation altered and distorted the Leicester branch most. In the early years, the WSPU consistently argued that class was unimportant, and all recruits were urged to leave any class feelings behind. But in reality, and despite the constant calls for working women to come and join them in their fight, they were considered relatively unimportant to the struggle.

Not only that, but throughout the summer and autumn of 1907 both Christabel and her mother were becoming increasingly concerned at the rapid expansion of the WSPU within the North of England and Scotland, some of whose members were not entirely bound emotionally or psychologically to the Pankhursts' family. Instead, many were independent socialists with ideas of their own and were more than willing to support Mrs Billington-Greig's attempts to further the autonomy of the new branches. It has been argued that the Pankhurst fears were largely caused by the influx of new WSPU members, who had never laid eyes on the Pankhursts or been influenced by them, thus they could not be relied upon to follow Christabel's decisions without question.

Indeed, Christabel herself was amazed at the lack of deference displayed by some of the northern branches. As she stated, 'The WSPU had been founded and led by mother and myself…We went ahead and the others went with us.' As it has been pointed out, before this most branches were, in many respects, autonomous, and in general were free to run their own affairs as long as the basic policies formulated in Clement's Inn were followed.

But first, this new and formidable obstacle of branch autonomy had to be removed. During the summer of 1907, Mrs Billington-Greig had sought to further Leicester's independence by drawing up a scheme that would allow it a provincial council, with a treasury of their own. Further, other evidence received by Clement's Inn convinced the leadership that a spirit of independence was rife in the North, and many branches challenged the number of paid organisers sitting on the WSPU Committee. In turn, the Pankhursts sought to counter what they saw as a challenge to their authority and promptly cancelled the annual conference, due to be held on 12 October, and challenged all who could not accept their leadership to resign from the union. Instead, two meetings were held in September where Mrs Pankhurst told the gathering that in future she would have no one on the committee who was not in absolute accord with her. Further, on 15 September Mrs Pankhurst sent letters to all the local WSPU branches informing them of the changes and asking them to support the National Women's Social and Political Union with a pledge of loyal support. In Leicester the letter was received with some dismay, as a few women resigned their membership, but by the time the pledge cards arrived it appears, through the continuity of donations noted in *Votes For Women,* that most agreed to sign and continued to serve the Pankhurst cause.

With the battle for control now won, the Pankhursts were in a strong position to stamp their hegemony on the union as a whole, and, as a result, not only were the branches to lose their relative independence, but they were now to be subjected to a shift in personnel. Consequently, at the beginning of 1908, and despite the

Many women chose to stay loyal to the Pankhurst family, despite the fact it became an undemocratic organisation.

fact that a coexistence between the classes had existed for a considerable period of time, emphasis was instructed to be placed on those women who had 'an influential position, both socially and professionally' to join the movement. Of course, this had been Christabel's goal for some time, but now a concerted effort was to be made, the results of which were to have dramatic repercussions in Leicester. Undoubtedly, other branches around the country, especially the industrial North, would have also been affected by the implementation of this policy, and to suggest otherwise would be to argue that Leicester was a special case with factors and conditions that affected only them.

In Leicester, on the one hand, while the result of this quest for women of status and wealth was to revive the older, sectarian aspects of class conflict, the branch managed to stave off the problem of desertion. Indeed, throughout the branch's early months there had always been a committed pool of reserves working in the boot and shoe factories around the town. As has already been pointed out, these women were active trade union members and had much experience of participating in local politics, whether through the WCG or the trade union movement. There is much evidence within the local press reports of early meetings to suggest that, at first, many of these women actively saw the WSPU as another form of female trade union and sought to use the organisation to promote trade issues, involving the WSPU in trade disputes like the strike at Rowsell and Sons in the summer of 1908.

Both Alice Hawkins and Bertha Clark appealed to all working women to come and join them in what they called their 'great fight for freedom'. Of course, under the leadership of such women it is hardly surprising that the local WSPU reflected the work they had begun in the trades council and the trade union. They had not yet fully seen themselves as part of a wider organisation that would increasingly have little to do with working women. Instead, they concentrated on the problems of low wages and the failure of the town council to appoint a woman probation officer. The motion to confront this issue was raised by Evelyn Close, a Poor Law Guardian who strongly believed that the interests of women and children probationers would be seriously overlooked by the appointment of a male probation officer to oversee their cases. Without doubt, this was of some importance to them, and they felt, long before the Pankhursts' sojourn into the world of the white-slave trade, that women's interests must be safeguarded within the legal process.

As they saw it, much of the female crime that was coming before the magistrate's bench was a direct result of women's social inferiority and their economic dependence on men. Moreover, the legislation that would improve working conditions and advance the social conditions of poor women would only come from them having the vote.

Consequently, until that time appeared women needed to be represented by officials of their own sex who could not only empathise with their problems, but who would also treat them as victims rather than offenders. It was argued with some passion that women were forced into prostitution because of their social conditions and their inability to earn either a living wage or be able to keep for themselves what little they earned. In Leicester, on the other hand, Alice Hawkins and Bertha Clark had lived and worked among the poor and had acquired real insights into the problems and concerns of the poor and repressed.

In Leicester, the forces of change implemented by the triumvirate took rather longer to materialise than in other areas and possibly were not evident until the second part of 1909, when Laura Ainsworth arrived in Leicester to take control. Consequently, for much of this period, Alice Hawkins and Bertha Clark were relatively free to pursue their own goals and policies, which, inevitably, meant trying to recruit and mobilise working women in large numbers. As a result, almost from the start, and despite the regular sharing of platforms around the town, the women from the different societies were never socially or ideologically similar and, in effect, were never in direct competition with each other for new members. Almost in direct contrast to other areas, the Leicester NUWSS was predominantly middle class and never really viewed the local WSPU as anything other than as an irritant that clouded the issues by staging media stunts. For them, the notorious behaviour of the WSPU acted as a diversion from the main issue. Completely taking the non-militant line, the editorial in the *Leicester Mercury* summed up the mood and feelings of the NUWSS:

'Mr MacDonald was again subjected to suffragette interruptions… the interrupters thus doing damage to the very cause they are presumably desirous of serving. It is little use attempting arguments with these ladies… otherwise it might be pointed out to them that conversions are not made to women's suffrage with the methods of the WSPU… Militancy will never secure the franchise. What it does is to strengthen

Nellie Kenny.

the hands of those who contend that women's suffrage would be a blunder.'

On a national level, Leicester and other areas were encouraged to join the protests and demonstrations in London and to assimilate themselves into the wider organisation as fast as they could. This absorption commenced almost as soon as 1908 began and was in direct response to Asquith and Balfour's challenge to the WSPU to demonstrate that the majority of women were in favour of the vote.

Leaving aside for the moment both the decision to exclude, wherever possible, working women, and the alienation of the non-militants, the WSPU leadership in London sought to field as many of their members as possible in London demonstrations. To this end, national and local leaders undertook long and gruelling lecture tours to try and recruit more women into the movement. In Leicester, mainly through the efforts of Nellie Kenney and Alice Hawkins, attempts were made to push the message into the small market towns and villages within the East Midlands. As one member wrote:

> 'Now is the time for the great mass of English women to simultaneously rise to the climax…We Midland women must do our share. We ought to be able to raise a strong force…to go and support, in person, the band of noble women who have borne the dust and heat of battle.'

Sir Maurice Levy MP.

Within the town, the Liberals kept up the pressure on the WSPU to show a popular will, and to this end the Government's message was again reinforced in Leicester, at a National Liberal Federation meeting held at the Temperance Hall, when Sir Maurice Levy MP said that he hoped the federation would not accept any resolution approving the principle of women's suffrage until the majority of the electors had expressed themselves in favour of it. He said that the proceedings of a certain body of women who had shown themselves so bitterly hostile to the present Government were outright 'scandalous'.

In Leicester, preparations for the meeting were hastily arranged, and Leicester, Loughborough and Nottingham sent women to the Albert Hall meeting on the 19 March. This large meeting, numbering around 10,000 women, had a profound effect on the women from the provinces; indeed, Alice Hawkins kept a newspaper account of this meeting for the rest of her life. Nevertheless, while some of the working women of Leicester had previously experienced the thrill and euphoria of a major rally, the Albert Hall rally began to bond the regional members together into a tighter, close-knit group. Excellent stage management around Mrs Pankhurst's empty chair provoked impulsive offers of money, as hundreds of promise cards were sent up to the platform as the excitement mounted. Mrs Pankhurst was not expected to appear on the platform due to her prison sentence, but during the day Herbert Gladstone ordered her release and she arrived at the Albert Hall rather late.

It was as a direct consequence of this type of criticism that Christabel Pankhurst began not only to mobilise the suffragette movement, but also to demonstrate the existence of widespread support through the use of mass meetings around the country. She later wrote that:

'The event of the year was our Albert Hall meeting. The first women's suffrage meeting ever held there and the largest indoor meeting for votes for women.'

At first, everybody believed she was still in prison, and when, at the last moment, Christabel Pankhurst announced that her mother had been released that afternoon the effect was astounding, and everyone gasped as Mrs Pankhurst climbed the steps of the stage at the height of the applause.

Without doubt, not only did these meetings give heart to the older, battle-scarred veterans of the assaults on Parliament, but they also gave the younger, more impressionable women a source of strength and confidence. In Leicester, young middle-class women like Isobel Logan, the daughter of the Liberal MP for Market Harborough, and others of high birth coming into the organisation, began to feel their way and, greatly inspired by other London militants, volunteered for danger duty. In many ways, of course, this acceptance of danger and the likelihood of arrest and imprisonment was a big step for them. Unsure of what to expect, and despite an almost unbreakable cheeriness, the rigours of prison life shocked most of them to the core. To some extent, Alice Hawkins had felt this horror during her first prison sentence in February 1907, although at the age of 44, not in the best physical health and less well equipped to deal with the situation she appeared to hold up better than some of the younger women that followed her.

The consequences, however, of such a shock had a greater effect on these young women and produced a more violent radicalism than could have been anticipated by the Liberal Government. The Government's initial aim had been to teach these young women a lesson, and many within the Cabinet genuinely believed that delicate young women could not, or would not, put up with the shame and degradation of prison life. Yet, not only could some of these women endure the deprivation of incarceration, being thrown into cells with common offenders, prostitutes and thieves, but the harsh realities of prison life also made meek and mild women of all social groups into valiant champions of an oppressed sex, with a deep mistrust of all men and male organisations. Indeed, this anger was to surface more obviously after 1912, when the local WSPU undertook a campaign against men and their institutions. As David Mitchell eloquently pointed out in *Queen Christabel*, Mrs Pankhurst led her cohorts into a dark Dickensian world of drab slums, poverty and martial violence, where nothing was more calculated to rouse militancy against a man's world.

Following the impressive Albert Hall meeting in the early part of the year, the WSPU announced that the union would hold a mass meeting within Hyde Park on 21 June. This was to be their magnum opus and the greatest franchise demonstration in London since the 1860s. At its height, 30 special trains were run from 70 different towns to bring in thousands of women from the four corners of the country. It was to be known as Women's Sunday, and throughout

No. 5 stall in Hyde Park. Stalls like this were placed all over the park, and Alice Hawkins spoke at one to members of the public in an attempt to get their message over.

Christabel Pankhurst in Hyde Park in 1908.

the day 80 women speakers, including Alice Hawkins, would hold meetings on 20 platforms. Without doubt, the Hyde Park rally was to be the provincial women's finest moment, eclipsing that of the Albert Hall meeting. Not only did they attend one of the largest open-air meetings for women's suffrage (*The Times* estimated that between 250,000 and 500,000 people attended), but later a jubilant Christabel Pankhurst claimed that the demonstration was the largest ever gathered on one spot at one time in the history of the world.

Leaving aside for the moment the rhetoric, the event was without doubt huge in every sense of the word, and met in full the demands made by Asquith that the women demonstrate a popular base for their claim. However, behind the scenes there had been over four months of almost frantic preparations at Clement's Inn by Mrs Pethick-Lawrence. Back home, the local branches began a series of meetings around the market towns of their county to try and drum up support for the demonstration. In Leicester, Alice Hawkins, for her part, stood on a wooden crate outside local factory gates, both during the lunch hour and the evening, and appealed to the people to join them in, what she termed, their great fight.

Of course, the problems for working women were somewhat acute. For example, an extra financial burden was undoubtedly placed on those women earning less than 15/- a week by Mrs Pethick-Lawrence's insistence that all members attending the WSPU meeting in Hyde Park in June 1908 had to wear the new costume of purple, white and green. Moreover, the cost of attending such

The WSPU march into the park. The Leicester banner can just be seen on the right.

meetings was enormous in terms of train fares, which stood at 6/-, accommodation and time off work. In order to offset the cost of travelling to London, in June 1908 Alice Hawkins and Nellie Kenney toured the county collecting contributions and donations to help pay for train fares.

As a result, many working women within the local branch must have felt a sense of isolation from mainstream WSPU policy because of their inability to purchase the necessary image. By studying the list of names published in the WSPU paper, *Votes For Women*, it was possible to deduce that the processions to London from Leicester not only decreased in size, but they increased in middle-class participation. The procession had just seven members attending: Isobel Logan,

WSPU narrowboat cruised the Thames outside the House of Commons. The message to cabinet ministers reflected the statement made by Asquith that he would support female suffrage if the WSPU could demonstrate that enough women wanted it. He, of course, reneged on his promise.

Jessie Bennett, Ada Billington, Eva Lines, Jane Wyatt, Miss Bowen and Alice Hawkins. However, it must be noted that despite the heavy demands of earning a living and running a home, Alice Hawkins managed to attend most of the meetings between 1907 and 1914.

Not only did time and money play a large factor in isolating many of these women, but also many had families that needed looking after. Throughout these years this was a perennial problem and, undoubtedly, played a major part in the extent to which women could play an active role. To some extent, yet in different ways, both Christabel Pankhurst and Alice Hawkins understood the nature of the problem; while Alice Hawkins sought to help and support these women, Christabel Pankhurst sought to remove them, if not from the organisation completely then from taking a more active role. From this time onwards, instructions were passed down to the local unions not to focus their recruitment drives on working women alone, and in order to see this measure was carried out Gladice Keevil was appointed to oversee both branches. This appointment was carried out from Gladice Keevil's regional office in Birmingham and was one of the eight provincial district offices created at this time.

Under Christabel Pankhurst's new directive, however, a greater emphasis was to be placed on women of wealth and position. This shift of policy from Clement's Inn was to have sweeping consequences for the Leicester branch and marked a significant change in the social and economic make up of its personnel. Under the guidance of Gladice Keevil, the branch, to the horror of some of its members, began a concerted effort to recruit women of the required background and influence.

One such woman, Miss Isobel Logan, had been a committed Liberal in her own right but had become increasingly dissatisfied with the lack of action by organisations like the Women's Liberal Association, as her resignation letter makes clear:

'To my mind the question of women's suffrage is so important and its continued denial so great an

Ada Billington.

Eva Lines.

Jayne Lavina Wyatt.

injustice to women, that it is impossible for me to belong to an association that does not put the question before others. For the same reason I am sorry that I can no longer resubscribe to your funds.'

Clearly what was bad news for the coffers of the WLA proved beneficial to the WSPU, for Isobel Logan was a wealthy woman of some local standing and often cut a dashing figure as she attended suffrage meetings in her motor car. Yet this conversion went much deeper than just financial support. Without doubt, close contacts with the working women of the Leicester WSPU had a profound effect on her, and soon after joining the WSPU she took employment as a bookbinder. In some ways this might well have been seen as a token gesture by a woman who clearly didn't need to work, but not only had she been converted to socialism and the need for working women to be independent, but she also argued that women should be allowed to enter the labour market on equal terms with men. However, this conversion to socialism was also tempered with a little luxury, and in August she invited Alice Hawkins and the Clarion Cycle Club to attend a picnic in the grounds of her father's house in East Langton.

In other respects this drive to recruit middle-class women was more than fruitful, as the branch was also able to recruit a number of women from the teaching profession. One such member was Jane Lavina Wyatt, a young woman who lived and taught in the Belgrave area of the town, and, although she was not to become a rebel militant in the image of others, she was a stalwart member and completely dedicated to the Pankhursts and their cause. Another recruit, Mrs F.W. Bennett, also epitomised the new breed of middle-class women coming into the movement. She not only managed to hold an 'At Home' at the Wyvan Hotel on London Road for Mrs Pankhurst's visit to Leicester, but almost from the start her organisational skills and the ability to co-ordinate and chair at scores of local meetings proved to be of immense value to the movement. Indeed, as an outspoken and confident member, she relieved the growing workload of Alice Hawkins and Bertha Clark, and, while these two continued to address the issues of working women, Mrs Bennett expanded the work and policies of the national WSPU. As a result, the branch began to grow more confident as more local women were able and willing to stand on makeshift platforms around the town to speak to crowds that could number several hundred.

In this sense, the London suffragettes' social make up and

ideology should not be seen as exceptional, in that they reconstructed many of the local organisations in their own image. Of course, in Leicester some local working women survived the initial metamorphosis, like Alice Hawkins and Bertha Clark, but others did not. On this point, it was partly a question of morale. The influx of relatively rich middle-class women denied them a sustained commitment to a movement that, at first, appeared to be an outlet for their own class objectives. Disillusionment and then apathy followed the Pankhursts' decision, but, more importantly, it was the working women's inability to associate themselves with a class that failed to understand their problems that alienated not only existing members, but also a wider potential group of women working in different industries in Leicester. Yet, despite the ramifications of this conflict between women workers and the new radical, middle-class suffragette, this was only part of a wider, more general pattern of change.

In London, this sea change was financially led, and all the reforms within the provinces were a direct result of this successful policy. Covering the period of 1 March 1908 to 28 February 1909, the WSPU's third annual report suggested that in the fiscal year the income of the union had nearly trebled, bringing its assets to a total of £21,214, compared with £7,564 the previous year. Further, the number of paid organisers had doubled to keep abreast of the escalating membership. By 1909 there were 30 regional organisers, compared with only 14 the previous year. The number of paid staff in London increased from 18 to 45, including the staff of *Votes For Women*, and, as it has already been pointed out, in the provinces this growth was translated into a further 11 regional offices being established in towns and cities around the country.

After the Sunday procession in June 1908, some members from the Leicester and Nottingham branches returned home to meet the demands of either working or running a home, or even both. However, other members of the Leicester branch, like Isobel Logan, chose to stay in London and await the outcome of a petition sent by Christabel Pankhurst to Asquith informing him that the union had met his conditions in full. Unfortunately, by 25 June Clement's Inn received a reply from Asquith's office announcing that he had nothing new to add to his previous statement of 20 May. The response to the Government's procrastination was swift and sure, and the reaction promised a lively introduction into the WSPU for Isobel Logan. On 30 June she assembled in Caxton Hall with the rest of the WSPU, who had remained in London to see which way

the Cabinet would go. However, by the late afternoon it had become clear that the demonstration had failed to impress upon Asquith the need for female suffrage.

Incensed by this deliberate refusal to act, Mrs Pankhurst hastily drew up a small deputation once again, to carry a petition to the House of Commons. Inevitably the outcome was to be the same as all the others, and the police turned away the small deputation only to be met by a much larger procession behind it. As the women crowded into Parliament Square, Isobel Logan and some other women attempted to make speeches denouncing the Government's intransigence but were quickly arrested. Despite being defended by Lord Russell, a friend of the family, and claiming to be a political prisoner, she, along with 25 others, was fined or sentenced to three months' imprisonment in default of payment. She elected to go to prison and not only refused to wear a prison uniform, but also immediately went on hunger strike. However, her protest was short-lived as she was forcibly stripped, redressed in coarse prison uniform and force-fed.

Outside and throughout the women's incarceration, emotions were stirred up, and the Government's denials of brutality did not entirely disappear behind the rationalisation they offered, and much public sympathy was generated. The *Manchester Guardian,* for example, lamented that 'their stringent imprisonment...violates the public conscience'. Yet, in reality, public support for the WSPU was rapidly disappearing. In the early stages of militancy, many constitutionalists had been impressed by the individual bravery required to flout the law and seek imprisonment. But the increase in militant actions during 1909–10 began to arouse serious concerns within the non-militant camp. Indeed, the adoption of violent tactics led to the NUWSS publicly disavowing the WSPU's new direction. They now argued that it was a poor policy, which merely annoyed and angered politicians without bringing them to their senses.[1]

It wasn't just the politicians that were vexed at the increasing violence. There was a real and measurable shift in public opinion away from female suffrage. In 1912 the *Anti-Suffrage Review* published their findings of a poll of 72,301 people. Of this total:

20,915 were anti-suffrage females
11,869 were in favour of female suffrage
2,120 were neutral

Moreover, it is also argued that far from the Cat and Mouse Act

Postcards from Alice Hawkins's scrapbook.

Lord Pethick-Lawrence.

Emmeline Pethick-Lawrence.

invoking much public sympathy, many members of the public saw their suffering as self-imposed and their martyrdom as, in some sense, staged; indeed, many disliked what Mrs Billington-Greig called the suffragette 'double shuffle' between revolution and injured innocence.

Violence against women suffragettes was not only prompted by a deeper social concern about the role of women within the family, but it also had a direct correlation with militant tactics after 1912 and the Government's refusal to accept the legitimacy of WSPU complaints. In many ways, this view is more than justified as many acts of violence towards women in the East Midlands can be directly traced to acts of militancy. In Leicester attacks on suffragettes increased after 1909 and little support against force-feeding was found. As one 'anti' commented in Leicester in 1911:

'The suffragettes cannot surely have realised what a solid wall of opinion they have against their demands. The reason given may not always be sound argument, but the solid wall exists all the same.'

Throughout this later period there were numerous examples of suffragettes being attacked in the street. Indeed, attacks on women, whether they were suffragettes or not, also increased. As the *Leicester Chronicle* commented in 1913, 'Large crowds assembled in the marketplace looking for suffragettes' and when they were not found, there were many 'unwarranted attacks on innocent girls around the marketplace'. Moreover, the suffragettes and their supporters consistently distorted the extent to which the Asquith Government 'with its panoply of law enforcement agencies – police, prison warders and…prison doctors – operated independently of public opinion'. In reality, Asquith's treatment of the suffragettes rested on widespread public support.

However, the rigours and hardship of prison life

for a militant suffragette proved too demanding for Isobel Logan's delicate constitution, and she allowed Frederick Pethick-Lawrence to pay her fine just over a week later.[2]

Imprisonment had been a terrific shock to her, and it made her realise the extent to which some women were willing to go in order to win the vote. And although she vowed never to return to prison for her beliefs, she continued to champion the cause of militancy through to 1914. For example, not only was it likely that she supplied the intelligence for the arson attack on the house at Neville Holt, but, at the Leicester Corn Exchange in January 1909, she vigorously defended the need for increasing militancy should votes for women not be granted. She told the assembled audience that the use of militancy was bringing success for the WSPU campaign. However, for the duration of her holiday in 1908 she contented herself with running a summer campaign around Tenby's Castle Square, canvassing locals and visitors alike.

On the strength of the Hyde Park demonstration, it was decided by Clement's Inn to capitalise on its success and promote open-air meetings during what was left of the summer months of 1908. Consequently, in Leicester WSPU members continued to conduct what was now a tried and tested means of promoting their cause around their county. The biggest of these meetings was arranged for the Nottingham July holiday fortnight. Thirty thousand people turned up to what was known locally as 'on the Forest' in Nottingham's racecourse, to hear, and perhaps heckle, an all-star line-up of WSPU speakers. Mrs Pankhurst, Christabel Pankhurst, Mrs Pethick-Lawrence, Mrs Drummond, Annie Kenney, Nellie Kenney and Alice Hawkins fought to make themselves heard above a hostile crowd.

Miss Annie Kenney

Practically from the minute Mrs Pankhurst began to speak from Number One platform, she was heckled to the extent that her speech was completely drowned out. Appeals by the Nottingham suffragette, Mrs A. Stevenson, were met with howls of derision and calls of 'What about Asquith?' Meanwhile, on Number Five platform, Alice Hawkins was no better served; both Mrs Drummond and herself were attacked by a hostile crowd and several attempts were made to overturn the platform. Entreaties by both Alice Hawkins and Mrs Drummond were met by such a

Miss Helen Ogston.

roar that all hopes of calm were abandoned, and when Alice Hawkins was hit in the face by a clod of earth, she retired from the platform and the fray altogether. Clearly, the earlier problems from December 1907 had come back to haunt them, and as Richard Simon, father of one of the Nottingham WSPU members, later recalled, 'Much of the rushing and attempting to overturn the platforms was done by [a small number of Nottingham] university students'.

However, Alice Hawkins had fully recovered by the autumn campaign and, while determined efforts were being made to recruit more middle-class women into the suffragette movement, she and Lizzie Willson continued to try and recruit working women into the trade union movement. Indeed, a lingering strike at Rowsell and Sons consumed a great deal of Alice Hawkins's time, and, when one of the pickets, Elizabeth Smith, was arrested and charged with assault, Alice Hawkins was incensed at the injustice and organised a series of protest meetings in support of the right to strike and the need to picket. Moreover, the matter was brought up in the trades council but ultimately, other than condemning the JP, little could be done. However, the WSPU had now made many friends within the women's trade union movement.

All it needed now was to be able to translate this goodwill into positive action, but, as the branch's leadership moved further away from its working-class roots, this proved increasingly difficult. In some ways it was a missed opportunity, and when the WSPU further refused to become involved the initiative was lost for good. Only the residue of distaste was left in the mouths of the male trade unions. They had resented this intrusion and believed the women's actions had greatly retarded good relationships between themselves and the Employers Federation.

By 1909 the movement in Leicester had grown sufficiently for it to begin to branch out and take its message into the surrounding countryside. Still under the all-encompassing umbrella of Gladice Keevil's direction from Birmingham, the message was to be carried far and wide, and in much the same way as the early campaigns of 1908. From the onset of spring, excursions in the manner of the Clarion Cycle Club were planned to visit the surrounding villages and towns on bicycles to put the message over on village greens and outside factory gates. Consequently, by the end of the year an independent branch of the WSPU had been set up in Loughborough under the guidance of Miss Elsa Gaye. Unfortunately, nothing to date is known about these women other than one local suffragette, Miss Corcoran. She was the daughter of a local doctor and often gave advice and lectures to the women on how to speak in public. However, this relatively small branch was able to grow and not only was it able to open a shop in Baxter Gate, but its members often attended processions in London, side by side with the Leicester women.

In Leicester itself, the group was keen to continue its work attacking local political events, and when Winston Churchill arrived in the town to speak at the Palace Theatre it was too good a chance to miss. They had known of this event well in advance and plans were laid that would attempt to catch Churchill off his guard. But since his last visit to Leicester in January 1909, he was only too aware of what to expect from the women of the Midlands, and, consequently, all women were barred from the meeting.

One Nottingham woman was more than keen to show her worth and travelled down to Leicester to take part in the forthcoming demonstration. Under the increasing influence of Gladice Keevil, many young women like Helen Watts had now begun to develop personally and were soon ready to face the trials and tribulations of battle and imprisonment. For Helen Watts, the romantic vision of women in full revolt expressed itself as the martyred suffragette languishing in Holloway prison, and, as such, it was only a small step for her to take to join the legions of women seeking arrest and imprisonment. From what she left in the way of speeches and letters, her conversion to militancy was a long and thoughtful process that took at least two years, but when she had made up her mind her actions were dramatic and swift, and she was arrested and imprisoned twice in seven months.

The first imprisonment occurred in February 1909 in London. Signalling her intentions to be arrested at the forthcoming demonstration in the capital to her branch secretary, Miss Burgess, Helen Watts travelled south shortly after the New Year to stay with friends while she waited for Parliament to open in February. Later, she not only recalled her motives and feelings, but she also wrote about her arrest and imprisonment in some detail from the prison cell.

'There comes a time in every reform movement when some protest action against the continuance of injustice and consequent inevitable evils becomes a solemn and sacred duty, not to be ignored without shame and degradation of ideals…I

Opposite: Selling Votes For Women *on the street.*

left Caxton Hall with a deputation about a quarter to eight. There was a great crowd outside and almost immediately I and the girl I was walking with were separated from the rest. We made our way as best we could into Victoria Street until walking was quite easy, and we went quickly along till we got near the Houses of Parliament. There the police were waiting for us. I got separated from the other girl and tried to get past the police about six times. At last, I heard a man shout out, "Let her through" and I was allowed to go quietly on. I tried to walk through the gates and then I found a policeman was at my elbow. Another came up and I was marched between them (to Cannon Row police station.) At the station I found the girl I started out with. She had just arrived. We were the only ones here for some little time, but they are nearly all here now; the room is quite crowded and we shall be let out at 11 o'clock. Mr Pethick-Lawrence has bailed us all out till tomorrow morning and we shall have to present ourselves for trial at Bow Street Police Court at 10. I suppose we shall go off to Holloway about two hours later.'

This picture is often thought to be Helen Watts from Nottingham, although there is no direct evidence to support the claim.

As she was given a month in prison for obstruction, she cheerfully told the bench that she had every intention of doing the same again at the first opportunity. Interestingly enough, her actions were not without their consequences, for her father, who while declaring at

Campaigning at a local by-election.

the time he was a supporter of the women's claims, had not committed himself to advocating either the militant or non-militant groups. However, with his daughter's imprisonment, this neutrality was not to last, and as the militant campaign intensified he moved over and actively supported the non-militant National Union of Women's Suffrage Societies.

Her second prison sentence was to occur in Leicester when she, along with Nellie Crocker and Mary Rawson of the Nottingham branch, travelled to Leicester to help Alice Hawkins and a few other militants from Clement's Inn to disturb Churchill's forthcoming meeting of the Liberal Association. As the hour of the event approached, two suffragettes from London, Margaret Hewitt and Miss Joachim, who was dressed as a cowboy, rode up and down Granby Street and London Road proclaiming 'votes for women' and denouncing Churchill's stance on female suffrage.

Meanwhile, further down Belgrave Road, outside the Palace Theatre, Helen Watts, Mary Rawson, Alice Hawkins, Nellie Crocker, plus two national organisers from Clement's Inn, protested loudly at their exclusion, but as yet with no force. For a time it appeared to most of the Liberal officials that the meeting would progress without interruption. But they had reckoned without Alfred Hawkins, who was standing in the stalls towards the back of the hall. Like his wife, he was a committed socialist and deeply believed in the cause of the WSPU, and, as a man, he was able to enter the meeting with impunity. Later, as a result of his militant actions, he and his old

Alfred Hawkins, Alice's husband, and Victor Duval, founders of the Men's Political Union.

friend Victor Duval formed, with the blessing of the Pankhursts, the Men's Political Union of Women's Enfranchisement in 1910.

Judging his moment with care, he rounded upon Churchill's call for support with 'Why don't they [the Liberal Government] secure the support of women of the country? How dare you stand on a democratic platform.'

Predictably, he was asked to leave without further trouble and, predictably, he refused. As a result, he was rushed by four policemen and half a dozen stewards, who bundled him to the door and ejected him from the building. Once he was outside, the protest was all but over; however, the women decided to hold their own meeting, at the Old Cross[3] further up Belgrave Gate, for members of the public who had been unable to get in. Roused by the meeting and possibly egged on by the watching crowds, the women decided to attempt to regain entry to Churchill's meeting, but in the following struggle with waiting police all seven were arrested, including Alfred Hawkins.

Alfred's poster awarding him £100 for being ejected from a Liberal meeting in Bradford.

In keeping with WSPU policy, all six women elected to go to prison rather than pay the fine imposed. However, Alfred elected to pay his fine and return home. This action on his part reflected the hardship and problems working people faced when taking a militant course. The Hawkins family did not have the same financial security as many of their middle-class friends and his wage was important for their upkeep.

However, once in prison all six women immediately asked to see the governor, Mr J. Noon, and informed him that they would not submit to prison discipline or exchange their clothes for prison attire. Strangely enough, although they continued to refuse to work, eat or to wear prison clothes, they were not punished by the prison authorities. Indeed, even when Helen Watts broke two of her cell windows, no punishment was forthcoming. As Alice Hawkins said later of the governor, 'He was very nice.'

£100 DAMAGES
FOR
ILLEGAL EJECTION.

At Leeds Assizes, on the 23rd and 24th of March, 1911, before Mr. Justice Avory and a special jury, Mr. Alfred Hawkins was awarded £100 DAMAGES AND COSTS against the Committee of the Bradford League of Young Liberals, for his forcible ejection from a meeting at St. George's Hall, Bradford, addressed by the Right Hon. Winston Churchill, M.P. on November 26th, 1910.

WHAT TOOK PLACE:—"When Mr. Churchill was referring to the question about the House of Lords as having now reached its final stage, Mr. Hawkins stood up and said 'What you say applies equally to the women who are demanding the vote.' He was immediately seized by a number of stewards, run out of the hall and ejected down a staircase with such violence that his kneecap received a double fracture."

Mr. JUSTICE AVORY, summing up, said, "A mere intervention, such as has been proved in this case, does not authorise either the Chairman of the meeting or the stewards or anybody else summarily to eject that person from the meeting without previous request to him to go. . . . Until he has been requested to leave and his licence to be there has been determined, any person who lays hands upon him and turns him out of that meeting and out of his seat, IS IN LAW COMMITTING AN ASSAULT."

LIBERALS! Remember these words of the Learned Judge and do not commit an assault when those who cherish Liberal PRINCIPLES ABOVE PARTY assert a Briton's right to Free Speech even IN THE PRESENCE OF A CABINET MINISTER.

Price 9d. per 100, 6/- per 1,000.
Mr. Justice Avory's Summing up (verbatim) may be obtained (Price 1d. each) from the Union.

Published by the Men's Political Union for Women's Enfranchisement, 13, Buckingham Street, Strand, London, W.C.

Hugh Franklin, a member of the Men's Political Union.

Interestingly enough, although the middle-class, militant suffragette had materialised in Leicester, there were some signs that the older, more conservative and working-class sections of the WSPU still exerted a restricting influence on the group as a whole. Women like Mrs Barnes and Mrs Lowe, wife of a local Labour councillor, were deeply reluctant to follow the Pankhursts further down a more militant road.

Indeed, when faced with the prospect of assault and arrest at Churchill's second meeting at the Palace Theatre in Belgrave Gate, one member proclaimed that it was hardly worth the candle. Speaking publicly, she mockingly argued that because Leicester's public opinion was slow to arouse itself, 'There was a feeling among local members against taking the course which would send them down Welford Road.' Nevertheless, this excursion into prison had an interesting conclusion. Dr Pemberton-Peake, who lived above his practice in Oxford Street, was also the prison doctor and met the women in his professional capacity. Much impressed by what he saw in prison, both he and his wife became active members of the WSPU, with Mrs Pemberton-Peake taking a major role in the policy and direction of the branch. Her arrival, along with Jane Lavina Wyatt[4], Ada Billington and Eva Lines, marked almost a new beginning for the Leicester WSPU. These women had, for a time, belonged to the NUWSS, but found the members too 'dowdy' for their taste.

Indeed, curiously enough, both Eva Lines and Elizabeth Frisby, later to become the first female Lord Mayor of Leicester,[5] recalled that the branch began around this time.

Clearly that is not strictly true, but it appears that some form of reorganisation did take place. For example, from the notes taken at a meeting at the Victoria Galleries in Granby Street in October 1909, Mrs Pemberton-Peake informed the branch members that the radical suffragette Laura Ainsworth had been appointed as new organising secretary. For some time previously, Alice Hawkins had astutely recognised the limitations of her organisational skills and, throughout the early years, consistently appealed to Clement's Inn for a full-time organising secretary in order that they could 'make great strides' in getting their message across. Consequently, when Miss Ainsworth, a dyed-in-the-wool militant, was released from Winson Green prison on 5 October she travelled to Leicester to take control.

In some ways she was an important member of the WSPU, and it wasn't until her release that any definite facts about force-feeding were made public. Not only did she attempt to sue the Government, the prison governor and the visiting doctor for assault, she also helped to circulate a poster depicting the horrors of forcible-feeding. In sensationalist detail she wrote:

'I was raised into a sitting position and the tube about two foot long was produced. My mouth was prized open with what felt like a steel instrument, and then I felt them feeling for the proper passage. All this time, I was held down by four or five wardresses. I felt a choking sensation, and what I judged to be a cork gag was placed between my teeth to keep my mouth open.'

Laura Anisworth, organising secretary in the Leicester WSPU.

However, she was only to stay in Leicester for a short time before she moved on to a new position. Nevertheless, these new recruits were to become the more radical, professional militants under the new leadership of Dorothy Pethick, the younger sister of Mrs Pethick-Lawrence. Dorothy Pethick and her companion, Miss Bowker, had arrived in Leicester at the end of a prison sentence for breaking windows in Downing Street and Whitehall. They had been part of a deputation from Caxton Hall to petition the Prime Minister in late June.

Consequently, because of their actions both Dorothy Pethick and Miss Bowker were sent to Holloway prison, where they subsequently went on hunger strike and were forcibly-fed for the duration of their sentence. The horrors of Dorothy Pethick's experience were later revealed to a meeting in Northampton. In a calculated attempt to raise the militancy within these stout and steadfast women, she told them:

A poster depicting force-feeding. This, more than anything else, aroused public support and sympathy.

'After 53 hours fasting, I was assaulted by six women and three men in operating aprons, who held me in a chair with my hands bound, while I was fed by a nasal tube with a pint of milk and eggs beaten up.'

She then declared that the doctors were unnecessarily callous, careless and brutal. After one force-feeding exercise, one remarked that they never tested her heart, to which the other replied, 'Oh never mind, I expect that is all right'. After a short recuperation, both Dorothy Pethick and Dorothy Bowker arrived in Leicester and took

Dorothy Pethick, sister of Emmeline Pethick, and her companion Dorothy Bowker arrived in Leicester to move the branch in a new direction.

up residence at 11 Severn Street. Without doubt, the strength and character of this brave, tenacious woman, Dorothy Pethick, was an important determining factor in the branch's future development. For many adherents within the group, she was the catalyst that was to bring them all together and bind them into a fighting group. From now on, all sectarian politics were abandoned in favour of the Pankhursts' extreme militancy.

Both middle and working-class women had found a champion in whom they could not only believe, but also under whom they could unite, at least for the time being. In the end these women became more willing and financially able to meet the challenge of a Government that had all but declared war on them. They were to become, what Lady Constance Lytton proclaimed at a WSPU meeting in the Temperance Hall in November 1909, 'hooligan suffragettes'.[6]

In other areas, too, the WSPU were becoming very adept at tracking and accosting Government ministers around the country. This ability to follow ministers was aptly demonstrated in early 1909 when Winston Churchill was invited to speak at Leicester's Chamber Of Commerce. The local WSPU, under the guidance of Miss Cameron – a Young Hot Blood[7] from Leicester – began a dedicated campaign to waylay Churchill between the railway station and his hotel. She appointed local members to watch both the railway station in Great Central Street and the Grand Hotel. But despite extensive plans, Churchill was able to avoid them. Only Bertha Clark came close, when she managed to accost him outside his hotel. By the end of 1909 the Leicester branch had been radically altered by the Pankhurst family. The process of recruiting middle-class women had begun, and the branch was slowly being transformed away from its original make-up of working-class women into a more professional, militant organisation.

Notes

1   However, in both Leicester and Nottingham there was evidence that this policy was not entirely supported. For example, in Nottingham the NUWSS leader, Helena Dowson, wrote to the London leadership regretting the public stand against militancy. She told her headquarters that many of her local members were militant sympathisers. (Fawcett Library, London Guildhall University, Helena Dowson to Millicent Fawcett, 10 Oct 1909. M500/2/1/284. MPLA.) In Leicester Mrs Bernard Ellis of the local NUWSS told a gathering of suffragettes that many of the WSPU members were their sisters, who were 'sincerely devoted and ready to suffer for the cause they had so deeply at heart'. *Leicester Mercury* 30 March, 1909.

2   After her prison ordeal, she retired to Tenby for a short holiday staying at the Worcester House Hotel. *The Leicester Chronicle,* 14 August 1908.

3   According to J. Wilshere in a *Short History Of The Site And Construction Of The Leicester Clock Tower,* the Old Cross stood on the site of the Clock Tower. When the site was demolished in 1575, the site retained the name.

4   According to a local resident, Mr George Motley of 17 Edgehill Road, Leicester, Jane Lavina Wyatt lived on Gipsy Lane and taught at Harrison Road School.

5   She was to be indicative of this new breed of young radicals coming into the movement at this time. Although she was undoubtedly middle class, she was also a committed socialist and worked for eight years as a district visitor in some of the poorest areas of Leicester.

6   This expression was first used by Mrs Pankhurst on her earlier American tour.

7   The term Young Hot Bloods refers to an article in the *Daily News* which described the young followers of Mrs Pankhurst as the 'younger more hot-blooded members'. This phrase inspired Mary Home to form an inner circle of women under 30 to carry out acts of militancy which ran the risk of imprisonment. *Daily News,* September 1907.

Chapter Four

Truce, New Horizons and the Expansion of Trade Unionism in Leicester

'What does any woman want except a safe income and two babies and semi-detached villa in Putney with an aspidistra in the window?'
George Orwell, *Keep The Aspidistra Flying*

For much of the period during 1910 and 1911, the focus of the WSPU lay not so much on militant actions of the previous few years, but more on conciliation. After the consolidation and agitation of the past few months, the Leicester branch were in a strong position to continue their campaign of harassment. However, to the dismay of many Young Hot Bloods within the East Midlands, events in London were to overrun the policy and direction of the Leicester branch, and members from both sides of the class system found themselves reluctantly at peace. But conciliation was not to surrender, and, while the machinations of the leadership committed the WSPU to militant inactivity, the local branch reflected this change in tempo in a strikingly different way. With the arrival of Dorothy Pethick in Leicester at the end of December, the character and make up of the branch continued to change. The slow metamorphosis that had begun around the middle of 1908 now took on an urgent feel as the influx of young, lower and professional middle-class women appeared to increase.

Again, it is difficult to be precise as to the numbers involved as accurate figures were never recorded, but many new names were coming forward, especially after 1910, at meetings, in demonstrations and subscription lists published in *Votes For Women*. By cross-referencing their names to addresses in local directories it is possible to identify and classify, with a measure of certainty, their social background as more middle class than previous members. Although the list is incomplete, it is a useful sample:

WSPU Member	Address	Date Recruited
Isobel Logan	The Grange, East Langton	1909
Alice Pemberton-Peake	21 Oxford Street	1910
Mrs Smithies-Taylor	2 Newark Street	1910
Jane Lavina Wyatt	'Fernleigh' Gipsy Lane	1910
Ada Billington	Birstall	1910
Eva Lines	Birstall	1910
Mrs Jessie Bennett	104 Regents Road	1910
Elizabeth Frisby	One Oak, Stoughton Drive	1910
Mrs Swain	130 Regents Road	1910
Mrs Daisy Brightland	'Snydale' Stoneygate Road	1910

In the main, from 1910 onwards Dorothy Pethick was more than sympathetic to this class shift and deliberately cultivated a branch of young middle-class women who shared her background and interests, and who would also meet the WSPU's fiscal demands. One such convert, Miss Elizabeth Frisby, deeply concerned by what she saw, threw herself wholeheartedly into the WSPU and, as a result, went to prison on a number of occasions after 1910. Therefore, it is possible to argue that what took place after the arrival of Dorothy Pethick was a cultural change brought about by the leaders at Clement's Inn in London.

Yet while this shift of social class among the membership does not in itself point to any single, simple explanation of how the branch developed, it goes a long way to explaining why it changed as it did. But it is also important to note that many working women, because of work and family commitments, found it extremely difficult to remain an active member for any length of time. Thus, in a roundabout way the shift between the classes was a consequence of the union's own success; in much the same way as success breeds success, middle-class women with time on their hands flocked to the movement to be part of an organisation that had brought fashion and radicalism to the fore.

However, the trouble with this somewhat mechanical assessment of the situation is that the changes were often intangible. But, undoubtedly, this large influx of new recruits transformed the social and political direction of the union, and, by their example, developed the branch into a more effective group. In fact, through the use of their relative wealth, they were able to furnish another facet to the branch that had been hitherto underplayed. Thanks to higher

Elizabeth Frisby. She later became the first female Lord Mayor of Leicester.

Leicester's Temperance Hall. This building once stood on Granby Street.

Opposite: The Leicester WSPU shop at 14 Bowling Green Street and below the modern shop.

incomes and, as a consequence, more generous donations to the coffers, the WSPU was able to hold bigger and better public meetings in some of the larger halls around the town. For example, in one meeting alone in the Temperance Hall in Leicester, *The Suffragette* noted that over £1,500 was raised in one night. Moreover, the use of this medium more than doubled that of the previous year and this trend continued through to 1914. Further, mainly because of the leadership of Dorothy Pethick, the branch became more professional in its outlook.

The dynamics of change allowed these women, with their superior education, money and organising abilities, not only to take control of the running of the branch, but also to establish an official shop at number 14 Bowling Green Street, right in the heart of municipal Leicester. Of course, the local group had used headquarters before, notably a shop in Curzon Street, but they were not as professional as this. Indeed, the shop proved to be something of a success, for in its first year of trading it made almost £117 net profit.

In other areas of the campaign, the Leicester branch used its time well and promoted the WSPU message wherever it could. In both Loughborough and Market Harborough branches were actively encouraged and secured, while Alice Hawkins and others undertook to develop and foster good relationships between the trade union movement and the WSPU.

As we have seen, it was the unfolding of events in London that drove the momentum within the provinces, and the period of conciliation was no exception. Accepting the advice of the less militant friends of the WSPU, both Christabel and Mrs Pankhurst announced a halt to the militant campaign and, as a result, 1910 was ushered in under a climate of conciliation, as the WSPU leadership called a truce to allow the Government to consider the issue of votes for women without preconditions or threats. Nevertheless, possibly because of his Government's impending clash with the House of Lords and the certainty of a general election in early 1910, Asquith undoubtedly sought a period of calm in the Government that might neutralise the threat of militancy.

With this in mind, he seemed to become increasingly placid towards the issue of votes for women and openly supported the moves by Lord Lytton, brother of the suffragette Lady Constant Lytton, and Mr H. Brailsford to put together an all-party committee of 37 members to fully consider the whole question of women's suffrage.

Yet, in reality, Asquith's opposition to votes for women was never more vehement. His objections to women's enfranchisement were based on a belief that the existing social conventions were 'natural arrangements' and there were no passing reasons to tamper with them. He announced to a rally of 10,000 men at the Albert Hall on the eve of the General Election:

'Nearly two years ago I declared on behalf of the present government that in the event which we then contemplated, of our bringing in a Reform Bill, we should make the insertion of a suffragist amendment an open question for the House of Commons to decide. Through no intention and no fault of ours, that opportunity for raising the matter has been taken away.'

He probably had other considerations on his mind. This speech attempted to indicate that the issue with the House of Lords had cut short the term of the Government and that a pledge taken some time before would hold good in the new House of Commons. As the evidence of later Cabinet minutes makes clear, he never really had any intention of allowing votes for women.

Therefore, this move could be interpreted as nothing more than a cynical attempt to dilute the threat of the militant suffragettes while he resolved his differences with the Lords.

As a result of this proclamation, the Pankhursts appear to have been completely taken in by Asquith's perfidious promise and unilaterally called a truce to allow, as Christabel put it, 'The new government to decide its position on votes for women'. In the meantime, the working committee drafted, throughout the spring and early summer, a bill so framed that it would hopefully receive support from MPs of all parties. By and large it was based on the £10 property qualification within the meaning of the Representation of the People's Act of 1884, and had it been passed into law it would have only enfranchised around one million middle-class women.

Interestingly enough, even when the Leicester trades council and the ILP refused to support the measure because of its undemocratic nature, the working-class members within the WSPU appeared to approve of the bill without reservations. Indeed, both Alice Hawkins and Bertha Clark defended the Conciliation Bill and put a motion before the trades council asking for their support. Although the council finally refused the motion, these women had once again demonstrated that they were willing to put WSPU policy before class

Lady Constant Lytton, perhaps the only suffragette to die from force-feeding.

interests and argued that any measure, however biased towards the middle class, would be a step in the right direction.

In the meantime, the announcement of the truce by Clement's Inn did not mean that all action against the Liberals would stop – only that peaceful and constitutional methods would be deployed. Consequently, the campaign against the Liberals in the first general election of 1910 went ahead as planned, as the WSPU attempted to 'keep the Liberals out' at every possible chance, and in Northampton a double opportunity presented itself. Not only could the Leicester WSPU mount a campaign against the Liberal candidate, but they could also grasp the nettle and attempt to once again form a local branch. Indeed, Northampton had always remained elusive and, despite early attempts during 1908[1], nothing had been established. However, on this occasion both Leicester and Nottingham sent delegates in an attempt to establish a Northampton branch. Consequently, at the beginning of 1910 Miss Burgess from Nottingham and Dorothy Pethick from Leicester, with the help of a local woman, Mrs Sabins-Branch[2] of Abington Park, Northampton, arrived in Northampton, set up a temporary headquarters at 13 Bridge Street and began a concerted campaign to interest all reluctant local women.

Adopting their tried and tested methods of open-air meetings around the marketplace and factory gates, these women began their campaign on 4 January but were met by a wall of hostility that threatened to spill over into violence. Mirroring the events of July 1909, when Nellie Crocker and Georgina Brackenbury challenged the local youths to a stand-up fist fight around the fountain, the speakers were pelted with missiles and prevented from speaking. However, some stirrings of interest were made among local women, and when Christabel Pankhurst arrived to speak at the Town Hall the following Saturday the meeting was sold out. However, she was unable to attend the meeting due to the death of her younger brother. Instead, Mrs Pethick-Lawrence took her place on the rostrum.

On this point it might be worth speculating that had she been able to attend, and given her charismatic charm, a Northampton branch might well have been established a good 12 months before it finally was. Indeed, the mood and climate of the WSPU campaign at that time very much suited the Liberal temperaments of many of the women who would later form the branch. But, instead, the meetings and debates focused at working women, for the most part, went unheeded. As one suffragette, Miss Evans, lamented after

Georgina Brackenbury.

speaking at the gates of Messrs Sears one lunchtime, 'very few working women appeared interested in my lecture'.

It is extremely difficult to understand the reasons for this apathy, but social and economic disparity certainly played its part. Leaving aside the later involvement of the boot and shoe trade union in campaigning for higher female wages in 1911, according to Don Stanton, a member of the Arbitration Board around 1903, Northampton paid the lowest female wages, while the cost of living was 10 percent higher than in other comparable places. But, without doubt, inroads were being made and much of the work done at this time was to hold the WSPU in good stead when they returned for a third campaign at the end of 1911. Unfortunately, Elsie Miller, possibly on the advice of Alice Hawkins and Lizzie Willson who had spent a great deal of time promoting their new union in the area, focused on the working women in Thrapston and Kettering. But, due to indifference within the local workforce, the promotion fared badly and valuable time was lost. Nevertheless, once the switch to Northampton was made a branch was finally established around a core of Liberal, middle-class women.

Back in Leicester, for reasons that are still unclear, during the January election the local union's electioneering focused mainly on the seat of Sir Maurice Levy in the small market town of Loughborough. Some of the newer, younger members would cycle over to Loughborough, dressed in their party's colours, to help the newly formed Loughborough branch in their shop, at 68 Baxter Gate, distribute anti-Liberal literature. On the occasion of Mrs Pankhurst's visit to the town, Bertha Clark recalled her moment of finding the new shop.

'Approaching Loughborough, my badge and the union colours of green, white and purple drew salutes from smiling strangers – a pleasantly significant tribute to the work of Miss Pethick and Miss Elsa Gaye. There was no possibility of riding unawares past the shop in Baxter Gate – the crowd around the window proclaimed its whereabouts.'

Unfortunately, the impact on the local population is hard to determine, but, after damaging reports of WSPU activity over the previous months, the reception they appeared to receive was harsh to say the least. On one typical occasion, a meeting conducted in the marketplace nearly ended in disaster when a hostile crowd pelted Dorothy Pethick and Elsa Gaye with orange peel and eggs. As if that wasn't bad enough, the dray on which they were standing began to shift and move around, until one of its wheels locked and they were unceremoniously thrown to the ground. Finally, unable to carry on, the speakers were escorted from the crowd by a cordon of police. Sir Maurice Levy retained his seat, but by a significantly reduced majority. From this distance in time, it might well be argued that the work done by the local WSPU was of some consequence. Their meetings and persuasive arguments might have influenced some sympathetic male Liberal voters to vote in another direction.

Indeed, the suffragettes did, at this time, have wide support among the electors and many were more than supportive of their cause. But, in reality, the degree to which the suffragettes were responsible for reduced majorities in by-elections is hard to calculate.

The extent to which people were influenced by the campaign can never be fully known or measured. Of course, the WSPU believed that the losses sustained by Asquith's Government reflected their efforts; as one West Country member, Mrs Blathwayt, noted in her diary on 24 January 1910, 'The elections are going against the Liberals and their sins have come home to them one after another.'

However, although the Government's share of the seats was reduced by 102 to a total of only 273, and the balance of power was now held by 82 Irish National and 40 Labour members, clearly other factors were at work. In part, it was a consequence of Asquith's declining popularity and a shift by working-class men towards the ILP. Yet, however real or imagined they were, the claims of the WSPU could not be overlooked by a Government that was hemmed in on all sides, and it was therefore only natural that Asquith had every reason to fear another outbreak of suffragette militancy. Indeed, although the Conciliation Committee had been set up at the beginning of 1910, little had been done by the Government to introduce it further, and by the beginning of May hopes of it being given a hearing were beginning to fade. Just when the situation seemed to have reached a complete impasse, a national crisis occurred that would change everything. On 7 May it was announced that King Edward VII had died.

The death of the king ushered in a period of political procrastination as Asquith attempted to overcome the political inexperience of the new monarch. Fearful that any delay in the Conciliation Bill might lead to further outbreaks of militant action, Asquith allowed Shackleton, the Labour member for Clitheroe, to put the bill before the house, where it was allowed to pass almost unopposed. In a Machiavellian way, Asquith and the Cabinet had again cynically used the bill to divert and pacify the WSPU at a delicate time. Completely mollified and ignorant of Asquith's true intentions, the WSPU continued their truce, although by late June it became obvious to all concerned that Asquith was employing delaying tactics. Without doubt, Asquith was determined to kill the bill before its third reading, and referred the bill to a committee of the whole house. He had deliberately allowed the bill to run out of time so that by November it was clear to all that the measure was dead in the water.

Paradoxically, the introduction of the truce undoubtedly presented the WSPU with the twin problems of how to maintain interest and motivate their members in a period of relative calm. Christabel Pankhurst quite quickly realised, with that intuitive insight that she sometimes possessed, that much had to be done to sustain and continue the high level of motivation within the rank and file. To this end, throughout the pages of *Votes For Women*, Christabel attempted to motivate and placate discontent within the ranks by a series of editorials that kept her finger on the political pulse…and managed to create an impression of suspense and imminent victory.

In Leicester the dangers of losing interest among local women was as real as elsewhere, and it appears that much of their organised activity dropped off. Of course, as it has already been suggested, it may well have been that local newspapers no longer considered their meetings and rallies as newsworthy, but the few scattered reports that do exist suggest that there was a real decline in activity. Consequently, the London marches and parades provided a great relief and undoubtedly helped to keep members on board. In Leicester, under the direction of Dorothy Pethick and Mrs Bennett, preparations were well under way by the time the first coronation march was planned on 18 June 1910.

The Leicester WSPU parade around the town in 1910 as part of the campaign to promote their cause during the truce.

After the drabness of the state mourning for King Edward, a jovial atmosphere prevailed as the Leicester and Loughborough suffragettes marched with over 10,000 women and 40 bands from Blackfriars Bridge to the Albert Hall. By the end of the day the WSPU had raised over £5,000. As if this was not enough, just over a month

later both the Leicester and Loughborough women were back in the capital, marching in a large WSPU procession from Addison Road to Hyde Park. At this suffrage rally there were 40 platforms and over 150 speakers, including both Dorothy Pethick and Alice Hawkins.

As the *Daily Express* put it:

'Twenty thousand women, with music playing and banners flying, marched in two great processions, converging from East and West, to Hyde Park on Saturday afternoon. It was the third and largest demonstration organised by the suffragettes.'

The effects of these meetings were of tremendous benefit to the WSPU. Not only did they attract large crowds to watch the events unfold, but they also made a great impact on the public at large.

Without doubt, it was from such occasions that the WSPU could be credited with bringing to the suffrage question a prominence that was new and fortifying to both militants and non-militants alike. Even after the pageantry of these occasions the Leicester branch continued to use their time well, and Dorothy Pethick, with the help and support of Alice Hawkins, continued to push the message far and wide over the summer months. Taking to their bicycles on Sunday mornings, they conducted open-air meetings in Syston, Shepshed, Castle Donington, Kibworth and Melton Mowbray.

By November, when it had become clear to Mrs Pankhurst and the other leaders at Clement's Inn that the Conciliation Bill was doomed, they organised what was for them a typical response. All over the country, local branches received the call to arms that they had been expecting. Indeed, all through the long hot summer, Clement's Inn had been preparing for such an eventuality and had collected a list of names that would make up the deputation. Consequently, on Tuesday 15 November Dorothy Pethick in Leicester and Nellie Crocker in Nottingham received a telegram from Annie Kenny advising:

'Deputation to Prime Minister tomorrow instead of 22nd. Collect members whose names were given. They must meet in Caxton Hall London 2.30. Very Urgent.'

This was music to the ears of the militants, and on the same day Dorothy Pethick, Dorothy Bowker, Alice Hawkins, Elizabeth Frisby, Cameron Swain, Mrs Iondies and two others left Leicester to join the deputation, each one having volunteered for 'danger duty'. Unfortunately, the Caxton Hall meeting was postponed until the

Friday, so the small deputation from Leicester had to kick their heels until then. Other volunteers from other areas had also arrived in London, and their presence was creating something of a headache for the over-worked staff at Clement's Inn. But help was at hand and Jessie Kenney wrote to Isobel Seymour asking for help:

'If you could slip up to the offices tomorrow I shall be glad, as we have telegraphed to a great many people in the provinces…They will need mothering a little if they have to be in London till Friday.'

In the end, Alice Hawkins and the others were billeted in Putney. Three days later, on the Friday, Asquith announced to all concerned much of what they had expected. Since talks with the Lords had broken down, all Government business would take priority until the dissolution came into effect on 28 November. While he was speaking, the women were waiting in Caxton Hall, and when no mention of the Conciliation Bill was made Mrs Pankhurst rallied her troops of about 300 women, wearing white satin badges with the legend 'Deputation 1910' on it. She told them that all 'other efforts had failed, and they must press forward ready to sacrifice themselves, even unto death if need be in the cause of freedom'.

These proved to be no idle words, as the impending clash with the police, later to become known as Black Friday, proved to be the most bloody and violent yet. The reason for this is not hard to discover and it comes in the form of Winston Churchill. Before this, police tactics on earlier deputations had been to contain the women with both limited use of force and arrests, but, on this occasion, Churchill decided to take a different view. Clearly wanting to teach the WSPU a lesson, he drafted in police from the East End who not only had little experience of handling such demonstrations, but were also renowned for their tough approach. Consequently, they proceeded to attack the women in both a sexual and violent manner. As David Mitchell implies in *Queen Christabel*:

'As the campaign lengthened and tempers shortened, near (and sometimes actual) rape became a hazard of the tussles in Parliament Square.'

During the six hours of close fighting, clothes were ripped and women were violently assaulted. Eventually, 115 women and four men had been arrested, including most of the Leicester delegates.

However, on the following day, the charges against all the women were withdrawn after the prosecutor announced that Churchill, the Home Secretary, decided that 'no public advantage would be gained by continuing with the prosecution'. In fact, Churchill was deeply embarrassed by the treatment dealt out by the police and intended to drop the whole matter with as little fuss as possible. Later, in the House of Commons, he denied that any fresh instructions had been issued to the police, but he indicated that in any future clash 'police would make an arrest as soon as there was any occasion'. As the testimony of Alice Hawkins later suggested, Black Friday provided the WSPU members with a strong argument against risking personal injury and public degradation in favour of breaking windows. To many women, window breaking, resulting in immediate arrest, was now considered to be a safer form of militancy.

The women were openly attacked by the police and some were badly beaten up, including Alice Hawkins.

Four days after Black Friday, on the 22nd, Asquith again intimated that should his Government still be in office after the next election he would give time for a bill so framed as to admit a free amendment. However, this news was received with gloom and trepidation. In effect, they believed that Asquith had widened the bill so much that it would have little chance of success. Moreover, Asquith then piled insult upon injury when he only pledged further facilities in the next Parliament, not the next session. Incensed by what they had heard, the WSPU, still encamped in London, once again proceeded to march upon Downing Street to demand a better deal. This time, however, police were waiting to make arrests, and at least five Leicester women – Alice Hawkins, Elizabeth Frisby, Dorothy Pethick, Dorothy Bowker and Cameron Swain – were again arrested. Again, the fighting was every bit as bloody as Black Friday, only this time they implemented Emmeline Pankhurst's 'argument of the broken pane'. As a letter to Albert Hawkins makes clear, the events of the day were unlike any other that had gone before. Alice Hawkins wrote:

'We went in a body, about 300 of us, to Downing Street to tell him [Asquith] what we thought about it. Of course, we were met by a large body of police, and I can tell you it was awful. The police were simply horrid, and they banged and fought like a lot of tigers at times. After a large number of arrests they eventually got us out of the street into Whitehall. After about an hour, I was simply done up and made up my mind to do something else…When a number of women went out to break Cabinet Ministers' windows, I volunteered to lead 12 to Mr Harcourt's house…It was easier to break windows than have my body broken.'

SUFFRAGETTE ARRESTED OUTSIDE HOUSE OF COMMONS.

Constables conducting a suffragette to Cannon-row Police Station. — (" Daily Mirror " photograph.)

The Daily Mirror *captures a suffragette at the moment of her arrest outside the Houses of Parliament, from Alice Hawkin's scrapbook.*

In court the following day, of the 177 women arrested, a total of 75 were convicted. Within this group Alice Hawkins and Dorothy Pethick were each sentenced to 14 days' imprisonment. In the case of Dorothy Pethick, she complained that, although she had been charged with assaulting the police, she had in fact been sentenced for obstruction. When told by the bench that she was to receive 14 days for obstruction, she bitterly complained 'This sort of thing', she said, 'is a scandal. I shall go back to Leicester and get more women to revolt.' It transpired that, owing to other circumstances, both women were bought out before their sentences were completed. Consequently, the involvement of the Leicester women in the events around Black Friday amply demonstrated that the WSPU militancy did not preclude, or even exclude, the involvement of working women.

By December, the second General Election for 1910 had been called. But this time the results were more than disappointing for the WSPU. Despite intense campaigning on behalf of Clement's Inn, the position of all the major parties had remained virtually unchanged. Yet, in other ways, Clement's Inn had much to be optimistic about, as Asquith had promised to make time for the Conciliation Bill in Parliament. This sanguine belief had been nurtured by Austin Birrell, who told a combined deputation of suffragists towards the end of 1910 'It is my own strong opinion that when Parliament meets next year this question will be decided.' Of course, the Government had much to be concerned about, and indeed Asquith never lost sight of the fact that 1911 was to be the coronation year. Ultimately, it is difficult to prove that Asquith deliberately pursued a policy of tricking the WSPU into a truce in order that he could contain militancy at such a delicate time. Yet, to all intents and purposes, this was precisely what he did. Even Nevinson, without the benefit of hindsight, wrote in May of that year 'Lloyd George's statement seems to be a mere trap and snare in a vain hope of securing peace for this year'.

Nevertheless, and despite the reservations felt by others, Clement's Inn believed that all looked well, and in January 1911 Mrs Pankhurst's New Year manifesto speech optimistically proclaimed that 'This might be the wonder year that shall witness the peaceful settlement of the long weary struggle for political freedom for womanhood.'

In Leicester, the branch embraced this new development with as much ardour as the national leadership, and Alice Hawkins and Lizzie Willson lost no time in making good use of the peace to continue their work as impassioned trade unionists. The extent to which Clement's Inn approved or disapproved of this move is unfathomable, but it must be surmised that there was, at least, a tacit understanding that they could pursue their own goals, otherwise they would run the risk of being expelled from the union. Consequently, in January 1911 both women sought and won a place on the town's trades council. Thus, while Alfred Hawkins was away in London receiving commendations from the MPUWE for his part in disturbing a Liberal meeting in Bradford, Alice Hawkins continued to do what she liked best and drew attention to the problems faced by thousands of women workers within the town.

These problems were, of course, nothing new, but since 1904 there had been a slow brooding resentment among the female workforce within the boot and shoe trade. Although these workers were, on the whole, patient and generally accommodating towards the union, they were finding it increasingly difficult to bring themselves to take a dispassionate and tolerant view of their inferior position within not only the union but also the workplace. In essence, they were torn and divided as their Labour convictions prompted them to be sympathetic and helpful to the general aims of the trade union. Yet, they were also swayed by other considerations that tended to fracture along sex lines, like the reality of lower wages and a perception that they were 'getting much less for their subscription than men'.

They were especially hostile to the fact that when the union had managed to negotiate a fixed wage for all male employers at a time of slack trade, unemployment and shrinking earnings, the union had deliberately excluded women from this deal. Of course, it can be well argued that the union was only being pragmatic in the face of strong resistance by employers, but what is more important is that it was seen by female workers as sex discrimination and such high-handed dealings did much to antagonise and radicalise the local women, as only weeks before the union's president had said with some passion:

'As women are now becoming well organised there ought to be some minimum wage for adult women as well as adult men…At the present time, the wages women receive is a scandal and something ought to be done to try and improve their conditions. We ought to try and establish a minimum wage of 20 shillings a week for all adult females.'

Yet despite this poignant plea, so deftly drafted, Alice Hawkins, with some justification, felt betrayed and deserted by her male colleagues. To all intents and purposes, she had run full tilt into the patriarchal oppression of women based on the tacit assumption that all women were viewed as 'ladies' and, as such, were treated 'to expressions of elaborate concern, while permitting them no legal or personal freedoms'. And while it is true to say that female domesticity was primarily a middle-class value and that it was less strongly entrenched among the poor, many working-class men within the trade union movement still clung to the image as a focus to deny women an independent identity that was not entirely defined by their sexual role. Unable or unwilling to accept women as economic equals, the trade union movement, while not actively suppressing women's claims, quietly denied their grievances and requests. This, of course, was not a completely isolated phenomenon, but militant women like Alice touched a raw nerve that could not easily be ignored. The actions of these women attacked the inner citadel of male domination, and by battling for women's emancipation within the workplace they appeared to be denying their very nature as women, a nature that could only really be fulfilled through 'sexual passivity, acceptance of male domination and a nurturing motherhood'.

Yet while this might have been a lofty ideal in the minds of most men, the reality was a complete antithesis of what feminists now call 'penis envy' and the belief that women wanted to be men, and while it was true that radical women 'had only one model, one image…of a full and free human being, a man', the truth was that many women were being forced into the labour market through necessity. For thousands of women in and around Leicestershire, there was little alternative but to work or starve. Indeed, the victims of sweated labour were nearly all women and, as such, it is little wonder that, given the impetus of the feminist movement developing around them, they should seek to improve their appalling pay and conditions. Thus, despite the good intentions of a few enlightened men, the trade union movement was, in reality, fighting a rear-guard action against the women to protect and ensure that men continued dominance over them. But, as one suffragette proclaimed in a speech around 1909:

'It is therefore too late to assert that women's place is in the home…No logical argument can be advanced against the justice of the claims of women for the enfranchisement on the grounds of their vast industrial service to the state.'

Thus, in essence, the trade unions had not only utterly failed to consolidate the potentially favourable forces of the women, but they also appeared to be completely blind to the dangers of not doing so. For, indeed, their indifference became the most powerful stimulant to what was to become a full-blown sex war within the union in 1910, when the issue of fixing minimum rates for women was again addressed at the national conference. Despite a resolution that was passed that bound all female workers to recognise a Board of Arbitration, no real progress was made in either getting recognition of their claims by employers or getting a fixed rate of pay through union pressure.

This intransigence on behalf of both the national union and the Employers' Federation pushed the women's patience to breaking point and, if almost to add insult to injury, the union raised their membership subscription by a penny per week. Predictably, almost at once the women strongly objected to the increase and argued that it was grossly unfair for them to pay the same fee as the men but be refused the same services and protection that they recieved. By now Alice Hawkins and Lizzie Willson realised only too well that a time of crisis was fast approaching when they would have to make a stand and fight the male indifference within the national and local leadership. In reality, they were facing a two-pronged attack on their position, for, in addition to the indifference of their male colleagues, they were up against the vested interests of the union's leadership, who not only sought to protect male employment and wages, but also held the widespread belief that women within the industry brought an unstable element to an already fraught industrial relationship with local employers.

Dubbed by her male colleagues in the Labour movement as a radical firebrand, Lizzie Willson had long been a prominent trade unionist in the NUBSO and supporter of female suffrage, but, although largely sympathetic to the WSPU, as far as it is known she never actually joined the organisation. Instead, she devoted all her time and energies to the trade union movement and, as such, alongside Alice Hawkins, implored women to join the trade union.

Indeed, as early as the middle of June 1908 she had attended a NUBSO conference at the Trade Club in Higham Ferrers Road in Rushden, to complain that not enough was being done by the national union to help and support female workers in the industry.

In conjunction with this assault on the high citadels of male trade unionism, both Alice Hawkins and Gladice Keevil undertook a series of meetings at the request of the United Trades' Club in Kettering to try and capitalise upon Lizzie Willson's initiative and drum up support, not only for women's suffrage but also for trade union membership. On this point it is important to note that in Leicester, as well as elsewhere, the two often went hand in hand, and although Bertha Clark acknowledged that the commitment to the movement was not easy for married, working women, the benefits once won would all be worthwhile. Thus, she implored all who heard her to support not only the WSPU and its campaign for the vote, but also the striking women in Leicester.

Throughout 1911 both Alice Hawkins and Lizzie Willson, because of recent anti-trade union activity by the Employers' Federation, implored the trades council to take action against local firms discriminating against female workers, but to no avail. At every turn the council rejected joint action to combat what Alice Hawkins had dubbed 'those firms that wage war against trade unionism'. The trades council always deprecated such disturbances and tried hard to discourage and prevent open conflict. Instead, its members complained that they had enough on their plates in trying to control the situation without the interference of militant women. Mr T. Richards, President of the NUBSO, lamented that, for the first time in the history of the union, a section had become adherents to the suffrage movement.

Alice Hawkins quickly replied that one did not have to be a suffragette to fight for trade union rights, although she no doubt thought it helped. Instead, she pointed out that they were quite capable of conducting their trade union business without the aid of the WSPU, even if the President could not conduct the business of the national union without the aid of Socialism. As a consequence, the women were increasingly isolated at a time when male trade unionism, according to Alan Fox, was becoming more socialist, and the lack of action taken by the trades council only strengthened the hand of the employers to such an extent that many women in the hosiery trade were signing up to the no.3 branch of the NUBSO. However, when pushed by belligerent employers, these women later backed down and, to the dismay of Alice Hawkins, left the union.

By 1910 the relationship between the sexes had all but broken down, and when a meeting was held between the union and the Arbitration Board, at which the union settled for shop statements instead of a uniform agreement to cover all rates, the women rebelled. As Alan Fox later wrote, Lizzie Willson's subsequent vitriolic attack on the then president of the union, Mr Freak, was 'so unrestrained as to shock all but her followers'. In some ways, this failure by the union at large to take into account the issues raised by the women signalled the parting of the ways and, while Alan Fox lambasted both Lizzie Willson and Alice Hawkins for waging a sex war that distracted the male members from the more serious issues of the day, the whole protracted and bitter contest merely reflected the desperate plight many women were forced to endure. For well over 20 years little in the way of positive gains had been sought on behalf of industrial women workers. Thus, the shock of the union's decision to yet again exclude women from a rate-fixing agreement evoked a quick response from both Lizzie Willson and Alice Hawkins.

In direct defiance of the union's instructions, they bypassed the Board of Arbitration and called upon the services of Margaret Bondfield to negotiate on their behalf. Like Alice Hawkins, Margaret Bondfield had become a prominent trade unionist and, for a while, had been attracted to Hyndman's SDF. However, she later rejected its tones of violence and revolution and joined the ILP, where she befriended Mrs Margaret MacDonald and Alice Hawkins. However, while the dispute between the union and the women continued, a potentially more serious problem arose that was to widen the divisions between men and women even further.

The root of the trouble occurred at the Wheatsheaf Co-operative boot and shoe factory in Wigston, Leicester. Once again, the employers had changed, perhaps at the insistence of their male employees, the system of payments to the detriment of the women. Incensed by their actions and the reluctance of the NUBSO to intervene on their behalf, Lizzie Willson instructed the women to work to a go-slow that consequently put the men on short time. This action not only made the men more hostile to the women's cause, but it also hardened the employers' attitude and the company made a claim on the Guarantee Fund[3], asserting that the women workers had violated the terms of settlement between employers and the union. Their claim was, unsurprisingly, successful and the union was subsequently fined £200.

Since little had been gained by the women and as Margaret Bondfield was still in town, Lizzie Willson again called upon her services to attempt negotiations on her behalf without mentioning it to the union's council, whom she condemned as being totally unfit to arbitrate on women's issues. This action broke all established procedures and was the straw that broke the camel's back. Unable to condone her actions, the NUBSO leadership did the only thing that was possible and attacked her leadership of the women in increasingly bitter terms.

In retaliation, Lizzie Willson, incensed at the union's lack of support and open hostility, passed a veiled threat that, should the union again refuse to take positive steps to address the women's grievances, she would form a breakaway union. To make matters worse, this threat was made public when a letter was published in the *Leicester Daily Post* signed Portia[4]. The author, and there is no evidence to prove that it was Lizzie Willson herself, pointed out that:

> 'Considering the very unfair manner in which the women have been treated, there is only one honourable course for them to pursue, and that is to sever their connection with the union and immediately form the National Union of Women Boot and Shoe Operatives.'

In turn, the union replied by suspending both Alice Hawkins and Lizzie Willson. To the obvious relief of many men, the women promptly left and, as promised, formed their own union. This decision to go it alone opened up a new era of women's trade unionism in Leicester and, as the women sought to start their union, women from all over the county flocked to join in large numbers. As Alan Fox somewhat reluctantly concedes, 'The extent of the defections indicates that resentment among the women was not confined to a few fanatics.'

Although the evidence is somewhat conflicting, the outcome seems to be that the women benefitted from this move, and the independent union successfully negotiated rates for its members. Indeed, by 1911 the Women's Co-op Guild reported:

> 'We hear with great pleasure that a scale for the Leicester boot and shoe workers is being arranged by the CWS and the trade union. A number of processes are settled and others have been referred to arbitration.'

Further, it also fought for and achieved better conditions for all members, notably increased benefits until the age of 50 instead of 40. In the end, the union proved to be something of a success and survived until the mid 1930s, when the personalities of both Lizzie

Willson and Alice Hawkins were no longer prominent within the Independent.[5]

This agitation, seen in its true perspective, was undoubtedly linked to a wider pattern of women's revolts during the long hot summer of 1911 that had little to do with the influence of the WSPU, though they undoubtedly made much use of its dynamics and attempted to translate this dissatisfaction into support for votes for women – or at least the Leicester branch most certainly did. Throughout the land, women had been in a state of agitation for some time, as they were swept up and carried along with the tide of militancy that had infected much of industry. In the east end of London, women earning from five to 10 shillings struck in what was later called the Bermondsey Rising. Because of long hours, low pay and compulsory overtime, the women poured out of the jam, pickle, perambulator and food factories to join the men (especially the London dock workers) in the strikes which were taking place.

In the East Midlands the infectious mood of female militancy infiltrated unorganised women not only in the boot and shoe trade in Leicester and Northampton, but also the hosiery industry as well. In Nottingham, women within the lace industries, for the first time, began to flex their industrial muscles and caught the trade unions by surprise. Indeed, had the trade unions been involved from the start, the strikes would not have occurred. Yet that is not to say that the unions

Striking women from Thomas Brown's boot and shoe factory on Humberstone Road.

were far behind, as both the women's section of the Boot and Shoe Union and the Women's Trade Union League, under the leadership of Mary MacArthur, sought to take advantage of this upswing in female militancy and steer them towards trade union membership. 'A strike of unorganised workers', Mrs MacArthur declared, 'should always be utilised to form a trade union among them.'

Consequently, it was against this backdrop of female militant trade unionism that the Leicester WSPU, attempted to use the industrial unrest to their own advantage and openly supported the women wherever they could, in the hope that they would become willing converts to the cause. As a result, both the Gillette girls' strike at their Leicester factory in November 1911, and the strike at Thomas Brown's boot and shoe factory on the Humberstone Road towards the end of 1912, attracted Leicester WSPU sympathy and support.

On both occasions, individual members of the suffragettes undertook the responsibility to support and guide the women in their fight. For example, in the strike at Thomas Brown's, where around 117 women and girls walked out in protest at one of their number being dismissed, Eva Lines, a teacher at Ellis Avenue school, took it upon herself to champion their cause and stood beside them on the picket line.

Although the strike at Thomas Brown's was less dramatic than the Bermondsey Rising, it was none the less typical of the intervention the WSPU was undertaking in the interest of good relationships. But this entirely reflected the influence and impact of Alice Hawkins, as this interest was certainly not seen in other towns like Nottingham or Northampton, where striking women were all but ignored by their local suffragettes. Nor was it appreciated by male trade unionists, who saw it as a political gesture rather than a genuine attempt to help the women. Not that they, themselves, were more willing to help, for, indeed, they were not. At least twice during 1911 the Leicester trades council refused a request by Alice Hawkins and the WSPU to support the Conciliation Bill. Instead, they sought to push married women at least out of the factories altogether.

As one Leicester trade unionist declared:

'The mother who is out all day and does not return until 7.30pm has not sufficient time to provide for her husband's dinner…The mother who stays at home is best, for she has time to cherish her children as a mother ought to do.'

Instead, the existence of this elaborate help and the pretence of mutual obligation has to be added to a highly-motivated working-class presence within the local WSPU and its rigidly collaborationist ideology, and, despite the fact that many of the original working-class members had long since left, their legacy remained in form, if not in person. Of course, Alice Hawkins was still one of the prime movers for this support, but much of her dedication and commitment to trade union activity had rubbed off. However, none of this implies for a moment that the new leaders under the stewardship of Dorothy Pethick had reneged on the Pankhursts' line; instead, they moved towards unity within the branch and built upon their merged strengths. As a consequence, it neither disintegrated under the pressure nor did it solidify into a group with one will and direction, and in many ways this was its problem. Without a unity of purpose, it later lacked the ability to become more radical and militant after 1912.

Nevertheless, by the end of the summer the Leicester union had made good use of the truce and had been engaged, since the early spring, in consolidating the WSPU's good standing around the county and beyond. For instance, from late May and early June the Leicester branch had been making tentative moves towards the southern part of the county and had managed, with the help of Isobel Logan, to form what was, to all intents and purposes, a predominantly middle-class branch in Market Harborough under the capable leadership of Miss J. Jerwood of Little Bowden Rectory. In tandem with this campaign, the events within the trades council and the formation of the INUWBSO by Alice Hawkins and Lizzie Willson opened up wider possibilities. Linked with the WSPU's expansion into Northamptonshire, they began a series of campaigns to recruit the women boot and shoe workers of Northampton, especially around Kettering and Thrapston, into both the WSPU and the INUWBSO.

However, the male Northampton branch of the Boot and Shoe Union was quick to act to dispel any unwarranted unrest, and by introducing their intention to seek a minimum wage for all female boot and shoe operatives to the Northampton Employers Federation in January 1912 they managed to keep the Northampton women on board. Indeed, the General President, T.F. Richards, toured the region and claimed that 813 women had joined the union within the space of a month and, by and large, women outside Leicester remained loyal to the male-dominated union. As a result, Alice Hawkins and Lizzie Willson found it almost impossible to recruit women into their breakaway union.

At first, the Leicester WSPU recruitment drive fared much better

*Advertisement in a
Northampton newspaper
announcing the arrival of
Annie Kenny to speak at
the Whyte Melville Hall
in Northampton town.*

than those of previous years and was deliberately focused on the Kettering and Thrapston area, where Alice Hawkins had identified those most sympathetic to the cause. At first, according to Miss Elsie Miller, the campaign 'promised well', and by the end of October 1911 a branch was formed in Kettering around a few working women in the boot and shoe trade. Unfortunately, within a few weeks her earlier optimism proved misplaced and the group fizzled out. Without tangible evidence, it is difficult to know precisely why the group disbanded, but one reason for this failure could be lack of finance. During the early part of November, Miss Hughes, one of the Leicester campaigners, appealed to her branch in Leicester for financial assistance but, in real terms, little could be done, and by the end of November the Thrapston and Kettering branches were all but finished.

Unwilling to give up on Northamptonshire completely, Elsie Miller and Miss Hughes moved to 305 Wellingborough Road, Northampton, to try again. Here the response was more positive and Miss Miller was able to report that the nucleus of the Northampton branch had been formed by the end of the year. From a report in the *Northampton Daily Chronicle*[6] it is possible to know that the first meeting took place at the home of Mrs Crockett, at East Park Parade on 11 December 1911, and was largely middle class in composition. Moreover, the group also reflected the wide spectrum of political ideologies within the town.

For example, on the one hand, Mrs Agnes Croft represented the Labour Party, while Mrs Collier, Mrs Ellis and Mrs Butterfield represented the Conservative Primrose League. The rest, like Mrs Brooks, Mrs Buswell, Mrs Gubbins and Mrs Beattie, represented the Women's Liberal Association and a variety of different

*Northampton
marketplace before World
War One. The WSPU
held several meetings here
to try and coax the
women of the boot and
shoe industry to join
them.*

charitable and philanthropic societies around Northampton.

In Westminster, the political twists and turns of a Government reluctant to concede the issue continued to keep the militants guessing, while preparations were made around the East Midlands for the coronation in June. However, this did not mean to say that, this time, the leadership had been

completely taken in by Asquith's rhetoric and, although hoping for the best, some prepared for the worst by recruiting militants for active service. In Leicester, Dorothy Pethick's call to arms was received with enthusiasm, and, in accordance with her promise to the court in London on 23 November 1910 to incite further women to revolt, she began to try and motivate the younger women coming into the group to take up militant action. Nevertheless, her efforts were met with mixed reactions, and by early March she could only report that four women had signed up. However, what they lacked in numbers they made up for with enthusiasm, as one woman's letter of acceptance makes clear:

Suffragettes are released from prison after a demonstration.

> 'I have decided to join the next deputation. Since definitely deciding I have been filled with a feeling of calm, so different from what I have experienced on other deputations when I felt that my "duties" prevented my joining. Now I have no duty but one, and that is to prepare for active service.'

On 5 May the Conciliation Bill passed its second reading by a majority of 167, and, as the previous year, it was promptly sent before a committee of the whole house. Despite her massive reservations, Christabel still managed to proclaim it a 'great victory'. Yet, within a fortnight, Lloyd George announced that no further time would be allowed for the bill during that session, but promised time would be made available in the next. This smacked of the treachery of 1910 and was duly greeted with anger from within the ranks of the WSPU. However, the WSPU did not immediately reinstate a policy of militancy because Christabel had been informed privately that Sir Edward Grey would clarify the situation at the beginning of June. Instead, Sir Edward Grey's statement of 1 June merely promised that the term 'week' would be deemed 'elastic' and that the Government's intentions were entirely honourable. Placated once more, the WSPU again relaxed and a 'period of high optimism'

WSPU banner-sewing meeting.

was ushered in as they continued their preparations to organise a large London rally.

Along with 28 other women's suffrage societies, a massive women's coronation procession was planned for 17 June. Headed by 700 ex-prisoners of the campaign, the procession included about 40,000 women, who marched five abreast from the Embankment to the Albert Hall. At its height, the procession, comprising gaily-dressed women with banners flying and historical costumes, stretched for seven miles. Of course, in Leicester the preparations for the event had been under way since the beginning of the year when it was decided to produce silk banners for the parade.

As a result, all members were asked at their regular 'At Homes' to help with the sewing and also to raise funds to cover the cost. In Leicester this was approximated at five pounds, and the first banner-sewing meeting began in late April under the watchful eye of its designer, Mrs Pemberton-Peake, with the sessions continuing on Friday afternoons between three and six o'clock.[7]

It is interesting to note the scheduling of these meetings, for they possibly reflect the continued influence of the new middle-class militant. They alone had the time and energy to construct the banner at a time when most working women were either still at work or needed in the home to look after husbands and children. The banner was eventually unveiled by Miss Nellie Crocker, the militant organiser from Nottingham, and stood about 5ft high and around 3ft wide. It was suspended from a bamboo pole and was finished in the

WSPU colours of white, green and purple. Across the bottom of the banner, the inscription read 'Always and always facing toward the Light.' Across the top, 'Leicester' was emblazoned in large letters and the motif of the town, along with the Wyvern, was displayed in the centre.

By late autumn it was becoming increasingly clear to the WSPU both in Leicester and in London that the Government was attempting to withdraw from its commitment. This belief had been fostered by Lloyd George's statement to the Cabinet that if the bill was allowed to pass into law as it then stood, the electoral register would favour the Conservatives. Instead, and with the full knowledge that any bill that included working women would lose the support of many MPs within the house, he attempted to widen the bill as much as possible under the guise of seeking justice for all. Conversely, this action set up a debate within the Labour Party that completely distracted members like Ramsay MacDonald from the merits of the Conciliation Bill.

Instead, their philosophical arguments that all ratepayers, regardless of sex, should vote further alienated the working-class members of the WSPU, who had, up to this point, remained loyal to the Pankhurst line. In all events, the debate was to prove academic, as Asquith completely torpedoed the Conciliation Bill by announcing that his Government would introduce a Manhood Suffrage Bill that would be free for amendment to include women.

This measure was never going to be acceptable to the WSPU, and, as a result, the different branches were called together in the Albert Hall, where Christabel Pankhurst outlined the next move by insisting that an amendment for limited female suffrage tacked onto a Manhood Suffrage Bill was totally unacceptable and that the Government must sponsor the Conciliation Bill if the truce was to last.

However, the coronation and the fight with the House of Lords were out of the way and there was no need for the Government to continue the deception any further. Instead, all pretences were dropped, and the WSPU again took up the militant cause, but this time with increasing violence. Consequently, the 10th Women's Parliament opened in Caxton Hall on 21 November with a deputation of Leicester women sitting in the stalls. Towards the end of the session, Mrs Pethick-Lawrence, standing in for Mrs Pankhurst who was in America, led a deputation from the hall to Parliament Square, where the usual cordon of police awaited them. However, although Miss Elizabeth Frisby and Corrie Swain were arrested for police obstruction during the ensuing struggle, Alice Hawkins was

Opposite: The Leicester WSPU with their banner and motto 'always and always facing towards the light'.

The Leicester women parade around the town in the summer of 1911. They are marching down Bishop Street with the Town Hall behind them.

not there. She had been told to meet a group of women at the WSPU shop at 156 Charing Cross Road. She, like the rest, had been told not to wear badges or insignias and to dress in normal clothes. Then, armed with bags of stones and hammers, supplied to them at the shop, they set out to attack windows of government offices and business premises.

In the end, 220 women were arrested, including the three women from the East Midlands. Alice Hawkins was eventually charged with breaking a window in the Home Office and given 21 days. Both Miss Frisby and Corrie Swain were given five days apiece for assaulting police officers.

With the closing of the prison gates behind them, not only were all hopes of peace dashed, but also all pretence of political compromise went too. Within the ranks of the suffragettes, no longer would there be any illusion as to the intentions of the Asquith Government.

Metaphorically speaking, the gloves were off and the war between subject and government would begin in earnest. For their part, the Government sought to financially cripple the WSPU and silence its

A postcard from Alice's scrapbook of the WSPU leadership.

voice through the confiscation of *The Suffragette*'s printing press, while the WSPU, on the other hand, under the direction and guidance of Christabel Pankhurst in Paris, were not only forced underground and out of the main debate, but they also became locked in a desperate guerrilla war with male society in order to survive.

The WSPU made the slogan 'no taxation without representation' a key point in their campaign in 1911 and undertook a policy of avoiding the national census, which was carried out in that year.

SUFFRAGETTE PROCESSION. OCT. 7. 1911.

Notes

1. Two suffragettes, a Miss Lambert and Miss Sidley, attempted to organise a meeting in Northampton for Emmeline Pankhurst to come and talk, but they were badly hustled and beaten. Miss Sidley received a nasty blow on the face from a missile thrown from the crowd. The mood had deteriorated to such an extent that they had to seek police protection to escape. *Northampton Guardian*, 12 March 1908.

2. There were two Mrs Branch's in the Northampton WSPU and it's unknown if they were related. The other one, Mrs E. Branch, was aged around 40 and was married to Herbert Branch, who owned a small boot and shoe factory in Henry Street. She became the group's organising secretary and had previously been an officer in the Women's Liberal Association. They lived at Hill House, Kingsthorpe.

3. The Guarantee Fund was established by the National Union of Boot and Shoe Operatives in 1893 to cover both the costs and damages of unofficial strikes against Federation members.

4. Portia, from the Latin *portitor*. According to Marcus Palatus (184 BC) it is someone who forwards letters, or of an inquisitive woman.

5. The Independent National Union of Women's Boot and Shoe Operatives.

6. One member, Mrs Butterfield, was married to the proprietor of the *Northampton Daily Chronicle*.

7. *Votes For Women,* on 28 April 1911, noted that the first banner-sewing meeting was held at 130 Regents Road, Leicester, and was continued every Friday afternoon. It was unveiled for the first time at the Girl's Friendly Society room in St Martin's on 12 June 1911. *Votes For Women*, 18 June 1911.

The WSPU on the London Road by the railway station.

Chapter Five

The Return to Militancy and its Political, Economic and Social Consequences

'If we women are wrong in destroying property then I say…it was wrong for the founder of Christianity to destroy private property as he did when he lashed the money changers out of the temple and drove the Gadarene Swine into the sea.'

Emmeline Pankhurst

Influenced by the rejection of the Conciliation Bill and the promise by Asquith to introduce a wider Reform Bill that would make Tory support impossible, the WSPU entered into what would be its final and most violent phase. Over the next few years to 1914, the movement, both nationally and at local level, underwent a series of reforms that would transform the character and composition of the union as never before. Yet very few at the time could comprehend the consequences these forces of change would bring, nor the effect the transformation would have on the members as they moved away from the semblance of a pressure group to something akin to an illegal organisation who fought a guerrilla war with the Government. These forces of change were both internal and external to the

A lone suffragette sells her wares to raise money for the cause.

movement and created impulses that can be traced back to the leadership of both the WSPU and the Government. Thus, it is essential to see this period in terms of not only how the Leicester WSPU had come to reach this point, but, more crucially, to explore and assess the role the antagonism between the Government and Christabel Pankhurst played in this change.

As it has been pointed out, the local union had already undergone a limited process of change from 1910 onwards and by the end of 1912 had become a highly-motivated and professional group of women, entirely dedicated to the Pankhurst family. However, the consequences of the return to militancy in the form of vandalism and arson were to prove potentially damaging to the branch, and indeed to the loyalty

Emmeline Pankhurst.

A member of the Men's Political Union is arrested on Black Friday. This is a postcard from Alice Hawkins' scrapbook.

Arrest of CAPT. C. M. GONNE. Member of the Men's Political Union for Women's Enfranchisement, Parliament Square, November 18th, 1910. "*Daily Mirror*" *Photograph.*

of some of the working-class women. Dedicated as these women were, the following years were to test their commitment to the limit. Further, not only did the leadership, under the stewardship of Christabel Pankhurst, lead these women into a full-blown sex war with men, she also destroyed any hope of political support at a time when many within the ranks of the Labour Party and the Liberals had begun to feel a measure of sympathy for the women and their cause. In many ways, the organisation was to be wrong-footed by its pursuit of Christabel's policies and, as a result, would be excluded from the very real political debate that was about to unfold. On the ground, the long-term effects of these policies were felt in a tangible way by Alice Hawkins and the women of Leicester.

While other groups blossomed and embraced the new militant tactics with much candour, the Leicester branch suffered and, although Alice Hawkins stayed loyal, increased militancy led to a further reduction in the number of working women wishing to involve themselves in such actions, and it also prompted the local Labour Party to withdraw from offering any support that they felt might help.

Although the blame for these changes might be levelled at the growing isolation of the WSPU leaders at Clement's Inn and their inability to devise a policy to suit changing circumstances, it is also possible to argue that the outbreak of militancy in 1911 was a result of an extension of government policy and an active desire to rid itself of the burden of the women's movement. Leaving aside the very real problems the Liberals faced in Ireland and the House of Lords, votes for women was not an argument that had been won in the hearts and minds of many members of the Government. It had become increasingly obvious to the Cabinet that the potential spectre of women hunger striking in lonely prison cells created a martyrdom of a far greater magnitude than the martyrdom incurred by imprisonment alone.

Therefore, to Churchill and Asquith it might be argued that the solution appeared quite clear: they had to discredit the WSPU in the eyes of the general public before the situation deteriorated further. For example, the use of the hunger strike and the subsequent implementation of force-feeding brought many local Government bodies to support the enfranchisement of women. In Leicester, the corporation, along with other industrial areas of the Midlands like Birmingham, Coventry and Derby, demonstrated their support for the WSPU when they signed a declaration in 1911 in favour of the Conciliation Bill.

In other ways, too, local newspapers like the *Leicester Daily Post* confirmed all too often the validity of their case and went on to say that 'Both time and the march of events are alike on their side.' Consequently, it was in the face of such overwhelming public support that Churchill had come to sum up the feelings of some members of the Government when he commented that 'We are getting into very great peril over female suffrage' and that, because they were unwilling to concede to votes for women in any real sense, he feared the Government would 'fall' over what he termed 'petticoat politics'. As a result, there is some evidence to suggest that the Cabinet took the view that, in order to quash the WSPU and other militant organisations, they had to destroy, in the eyes of the general public, the suffragettes' good standing once and for all.

To this end, it seemed to many, including one local political commentator, more than likely that Hobhouse's 'The burning of Nottingham Castle' speech in Bristol was used as a stalkinghorse to incite women to further acts of violence.[1] As Charles Hickling pointed out in the *Nottingham Daily Express*:

'The recent attacks on buildings and letter boxes seem to have arisen from a remark by a Cabinet Minister…and the challenger is not free from blame.'

Indeed, not only would the Government have an ideal excuse to arrest and imprison the leaders, but they could also claim, with some justification, the moral high ground in the knowledge that any feelings of public sympathy would melt away at the destruction of private property. To some extent, this view proved entirely correct, and after

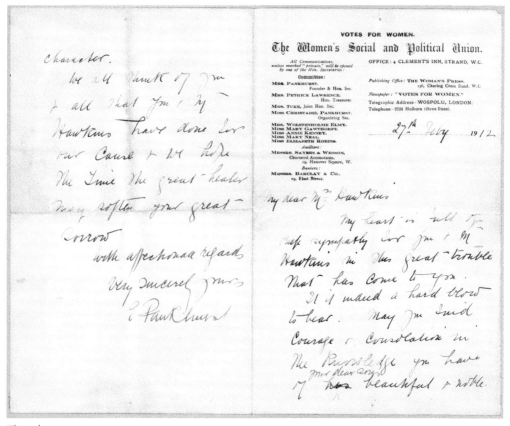

This telegram was sent to Alice Hawkins from Emmeline Pankhurst on the death of her son in 1912. Mrs Pankhurst shows great feeling for Alice as she had also just recently lost her son.

the destruction of letters in pillar boxes in both Nottingham and Leicester in 1912 the WSPU were swamped with cries of outrage and protest. In Leicester, Gladys Hazel, the new area organiser based in Birmingham, was forced on to the defensive and attempted to justify their actions by arguing that the attacks were symptomatic of the strong feelings prevalent among supporters of the suffrage movement, borne out of years of frustration and the way they had been treated by the Government. She further pointed out that in 40 years of constitutional agitation nothing had been accomplished, and if the WSPU were forced to unconstitutional methods people should not be too surprised.

However, despite the force of her arguments, she might well have saved her breath as these new acts of militancy were, in the main, lost on the general public; they were collectively shocked and outraged at the change of policy. Indeed, it was suggested locally that the women be publicly flogged. Responding to this call, one woman, Miss Margaret Haly, indignantly replied that if she were then that might help public opinion and put forward the view that they were 'fighting for the vote…and only by smashing windows and damaging letters can we convince the Government that we are in earnest'.

Although this process of change and the increasing use of vandalism as a weapon was possibly Government-led, it most certainly could not have occurred without the growing erratic behaviour of Christabel Pankhurst, who had consistently demonstrated 'a lack of political insight and even common sense', as she oscillated between militancy and conciliation. But, by the end of 1912, incensed by Asquith's obstructionism, she had returned to the war against the Liberals with a renewed vigour that gave little thought to the consequences her actions would have on the union. At first, to many WSPU members around the country the prospect of further militancy proved appealing and the offices of the union were again flooded with pledges of support in any militant action. In Leicester, the news of further militancy appears to have been received with some delight and several members of the Young Hot Blood Club, undeterred by arrests the previous year, enrolled for active service in the coming fight. Undoubtedly, this kind of response was, by and large, not unusual and only serves to demonstrate the often insular, single-mindedness of many of the Pankhurst followers. However, after doing her bit the year before, Alice Hawkins declined to volunteer and retired to take a back seat.

Christabel Pankhurst's militancy, nevertheless, brought into play the young, unmarried and middle-class hot blood radicals like Elizabeth Frisby and Cameron Swain. On the whole, they were more than willing to increase direct action within the organisation. Indeed, Miss Cameron Swain, Mrs Bennett and her daughter, Dorothy, volunteered for active service by telegram, and by 4 March they found themselves at the Albert Hall in London to hear Mrs Pankhurst inform them that 'the argument of the stone, that time-honoured official political argument' was now official WSPU policy. Interestingly enough, while this meeting was taking place, other Leicester women were preparing to take the Government by surprise and struck without warning in the West End of London. Only a quarter of an hour before the shops were due to close, young women strolling among the late-night shoppers suddenly produced from the depths of muffs and bags a large quantity of hammers and stones, and 'from every part of the crowds and brilliantly lighted streets came the crash of splintered glass'.

Among those arrested was a young Leicester militant who entirely

The Leicester WSPU were at the fore in the smashing of windows in London's West End.

reflected the new ethos of Christabel's ideal. Miss Cameron Swain, daughter of Mrs Cornelian Swain[2] of Regents Street, had been arrested twice in November 1911 and was now detained again, but this time she was sentenced to four months hard labour for breaking windows in New Bond Street.[3] True to form, immediately upon being placed in prison she went on hunger strike and was subjected to the horrors of force-feeding during her sentence. However, such deeds did not go unnoticed by the national leadership, and when Dorothy Pethick, possibly because of the growing friction between her sister and Christabel Pankhurst, later announced that she intended to step down, Cameron Swain was appointed temporary organising secretary for the Leicester branch in June 1912.

However, their radical enthusiasm was to cause wide-spread problems for the organisation as a whole. Many working women within the Leicester branch were alienated by the increasing use of violence and vandalism and they began to leave the organisation in increasing numbers. Arguably, in this way dissent was controlled and it allowed the branch to become more middle-class based. Yet, while many of Christabel Pankhurst's supporters, both in and out of the WSPU, had come to realise that she had become intoxicated with power and in reality, by the end of 1911, needed little excuse to resort to further acts of vandalism or arson, she was, of course, not entirely without vision and recognised quite quickly that Hobhouse's declaration would have 'a decisive effect on the future course of the women's suffrage movement'. But to what extent these changes would help or hinder the cause, she remained uncertain.

However, although Christabel was neither 'ignorant nor stupid', she often lacked the Machiavellian arts so adeptly practised by Asquith and the Cabinet, and from the onset of renewed militancy she not only willingly and unwillingly subjected the movement to splits and dissension by her intransigence to seek a more diplomatic route, but she also isolated the WSPU from any worthwhile debate. Yet, that is not to say that the Government would have been more accommodating had they continued their truce – far from it. However, another path lay open to her in the policies formulated by the Pethick-Lawrences, and that was to continue militant action within the bounds of public support.

For their part, the Pethick-Lawrences were deeply alarmed at the change of events. They reasoned, quite rightly, that if the WSPU took Christabel's path it would not only alienate the movement from public support, but it would practically drive the union underground. Instead, they argued, with some justification, that because the organisation had never been in such a strong position as it then was, Christabel should return from Paris to challenge the Government and allow the WSPU to mount a campaign 'which would restrict the ability of the Government to act…and this would lead to its ignominious defeat'. However, Christabel refused the advice given and continued her self-imposed exile in France, where, removed from the heart of the movement, she appeared to grow more and more nervous at her position within the WSPU. Deeply suspicious of Sylvia's ambitions on the one hand, and the Pethick-Lawrences' conciliatory approach to militancy on the other, she began a series of measures that would keep the WSPU within her influence and protect the organisation from the 'new elements…who would put peace or party politics, or both, before votes for women'.

In effect, this not only meant reorganising the branches during the autumn of 1912 into larger areas or groups, but it also meant removing from positions of influence any member of the WSPU who was not totally committed to her or her mother's decisions, and, almost by default, this meant the Pethick-Lawrences and Sylvia Pankhurst on a national level, and at a local level the leaders of the branches in Leicester and Nottingham. In both towns, the leadership of the branches was controlled by blood relations of the Pethick-Lawrences. For instance, in Nottingham Nellie Crocker was a cousin of Emmeline Pethick-Lawrence, while in Leicester Dorothy Pethick was, of course, her sister.

As a result of this infighting, both Nellie Crocker and Dorothy Pethick announced they intended to step down as organisers and in doing so created a crisis of leadership that allowed both branches to fall into a period of uncertainty and inactivity. However, to counter any break up of the provincial branches, both the Nottingham and Leicester group – with its offshoots in Loughborough and Market Harborough – for reasons of 'putting the branch on a firm financial footing', were brought into one large local union under the direct control of Gladys Hazel[4] in Birmingham, with Cameron Swain acting as local leader in Leicester and Charlotte Marsh in Nottingham.

On the face of it, this statement of putting the branch on a more firm financial footing was not entirely without foundation; indeed,

Charlotte Marsh.

throughout the summer of 1912 there were many rumours abound that the WSPU were suffering from a lack of motivation, primarily due to Christabel's absence from Britain and Mrs Pankhurst's constant visits to prison.

Consequently, by the middle of 1913 the *Daily Mail* had published an article that suggested the WSPU were suffering financially from a declining membership, poor administration and disorganisation. In some ways, this observation appeared to be correct, in that throughout this period much was made by the WSPU of the need for local branches to raise more and more cash to go towards what they called their 'war chest'. But, regardless of any truth in these interpretations, the changes did bring about a period of instability within the organisation. Whether this was also true elsewhere is hard to say, but for the Leicester branch it appears to be a period of much upheaval, managing at least four different leaders until the arrival of Kitty Marion in May 1914.

Perhaps the greatest consequence of Christabel Pankhurst's forced exile in Paris, besides the growth in her paranoia most noted by Henry Nevinson,[5] was its effect upon the local branches. Out of touch with the leadership, and for the most part left to the ad hoc policies of the local organisers, an increasing strain was placed upon their loyalty and commitment to stay faithful to the Pankhurst line. And now, at the beginning of 1913, their allegiance was again strained and tested, and for many a choice between the church and the WSPU was now needed. Yet, for her part, increasingly isolated and perhaps a little fearful of her own position within the WSPU, she began, with the expressed desire to bolster a flagging campaign, a moral crusade that was, through the assault on the church, to test and try the patience of all but the dedicated few.

While her religious feelings were conventionally expressed in much of the earlier campaigns, her later attacks on the established church suggest a religious experience more powerful and more private than conventional piety. Indeed, at her instigation, within the WSPU was the development of an almost quasi-religious element to their campaign. Of course, this was not really a new angle, as many local women, notably the Nottingham suffragette Penelope,[6] had taken this line for some years and she often laced her message with religious connotations. In the *Nottingham Guardian*, for example, Penelope argued that:

'The militant suffragettes are accounted "she-devils" today, but tomorrow they will be classed with the ever increasing number of saints who, in spite of their faults, have given up all temporal happiness and peace, wealth, life for the sake of justice, righteousness and truth.'

But now a sinister fundamentalism had begun to creep in that was wholly puritanical and, while proclaiming themselves as Church Militants, a reference to the zealous Jesuits in Counter-Reformation Spain, the WSPU systematically set about isolating the fragile support many church-goers felt able to give to the movement. From the middle of 1913 onwards, the WSPU, under the direction of Christabel in Paris, were increasingly determined to divorce themselves from individual men or male organisations and this, by default of course, meant the church. Christabel believed 'Women would become conscious of their own worth only through independence from men'; this was the most important plank in Christabel's policies during the latter years of militancy. In contrast, during the WSPU's early years many church leaders openly supported Christabel Pankhurst's line on male chastity and welcomed, at first, the debate 'The Great Scourge' would bring. Even while disputing her figures[7] they still lauded her stance on the white slave trade, a euphemism for prostitution, and the economic and social deprivation of many women, especially working women, who suffered at the hands of men. Indeed, many leading clergy praised her for her magnificent courage in fighting the hideous monster of sexual depravity and disease.

In many ways, Christabel Pankhurst was engaging herself in the debate and campaigns that focused around sexual morality, which were developed in order to define femininity, sex and morality in relation to political activity. To this end, Christabel sought to treat what she saw as a conspiracy of silence regarding the transmission of venereal disease among women. By linking VD as the cause of physical, mental and moral degeneracy which, in turn, resulted in race suicide, she condemned men in general and vindicated the purity of women by shifting the blame of racial degeneracy from women to men. For Christabel Pankhurst, it was important to show that men themselves were responsible for the nation's poor health.

By doing this, Christabel, in line with other feminists at this time, constructed a framework in which to understand women's subordinate position within society and, more importantly, the means for its eradication. Feminists drew on the ideology of female moral superiority and altruistic maternity to claim a position from which to enter the public world as moral missionaries and to insist on a right to political status.

But now, Christabel sought to eradicate women's subordinate position by taking the debate a step forward, challenging the belief that women were not disadvantaged by nature but by a predominately male culture. Now, in the interest of notoriety and publicity, she went further and advocated not only complete forced male chastity, but also a complete break from all male organisations, especially the church. Although she may have blamed male culture within the church for women's inferiority, she nevertheless drew upon the language and imagery of that culture for attacking, perhaps, the only male organisation which gave women a voice. Using religious terminology, in her 'appeal to God' she attacked the notion that despite the fact that many of the 'finest among the clergy' were supportive of the women in their noble crusade, the church on the whole was not and it had failed the nation in a great crisis, she went on that by forgetting that its own seed was the blood of the martyrs, it has no pity for the martyrs of the present day.

Inside St Mark's Church on Belgrave Road. The back painting, The Triumph of the Apotheosis, *was commissioned in 1910 by the Revd Donaldson from the Scottish painter Eadie Reid. Representatives of the WSPU and trade unions from all over England were present at the dedication. Also, a local legend claims that members of the WSPU and local trade unionists posed for the painting.*

In some respects she was right, as many church leaders had been more than willing to support the women and their cause and were equally indignant at the use of force-feeding and the subsequent Cat and Mouse Act.[8] In Lincolnshire, for instance, prompted by the Nottingham WSPU, even the Bishop of Lincoln made clear his feelings on the matter when he published a letter in *The Times*, which read:

'Methods of repression and expedients like the Cat and Mouse Act would deserve only ridicule, were it not for the suffering they involve. The only sane and lasting remedy for the present discontents is truly Liberal legislation; that is the extension of liberty through the franchise.'

In Leicester the support was much the same, and the Reverend Donaldson, before taking up the post at Westminster Abbey, had long championed and supported women's rights by sharing, shoulder to shoulder, the platforms of both the WSPU and the

NUWSS, and likewise protested and condemned the Government in its actions. As a committed socialist and Christian, he had often talked about the stress and poverty low wages caused for women, and as a result had been much interested in the formation of the WSPU in Leicester. Attracted to the ideals and direction Alice Hawkins gave to the branch, he supported the movement as much as possible and often allowed his church rooms to be used by the WSPU.

Within the local WSPU itself, church support was paramount, as many local women were active in church matters as well as the militant campaign. Not only that, but church activists were also militants and many formed their own organisation to campaign for the vote alongside the WSPU. And, without doubt, some of these church organisations did much in the way of keeping religious bodies on board.

In Leicester the link between the church and WSPU is less easy to define and as far as it can be seen, beyond the normal religious practice of the time, little contact was made between them. Indeed, little evidence survives to suggest that the local women ever used religious terminology in their speeches. Instead, they appeared to concentrate their energies on demanding the vote in the political arena, focusing on the social and economical rather than the spiritual. Christabel Pankhurst's moral crusade spoke out in favour of *The Great Scourge,* but their concern was mainly directed at the plight of women rather than targeting the double standards of men, as one member said in the spring of 1914, 'The root cause of all evil is not only the double standards of morality for men and women, but also the subjection and underpayment of women.'

Yet here was the paradox. While the WSPU were actively seeking the support of the Church of England and other free churches within the East Midlands at least, the national leadership undertook a two-pronged offensive against the national church body and not only attacked church leaders verbally, but also began a campaign of church disruption that resulted in the destruction of some churches by fire. Yet, despite the impending split, the schism between the church and the militant suffragettes was slow to materialise in Leicester, and in local branches members continued to see themselves as part of a wider moral crusade that included the church as well.

At first, according to Sylvia Pankhurst, the policy of disrupting church services was begun as a protest against the Cat and Mouse Act, but it was later extended to include the chanting of prayers for hunger strikers at churches around the country, the first of which was carried out in St Paul's in London in August 1913, when a group of women, in time with the litany chant, sang out, 'Save Emmeline Pankhurst, save her, save her.' At this stage, the manner of the protest was something of a novelty, and although the police were called the women were not ejected. However, as the protests increased and they lost their novel appeal, the mood of the congregations changed and women were physically attacked.

While there were no noted church interruptions in Leicester, matters took a different turn in Nottingham when church protests began around three months later, when five local suffragettes interrupted the main service in St Mary's Church, Nottingham, by chanting in time to the religious litany, 'Oh God save Annie Kenney, Sylvia Pankhurst and all the women who are persecuted and suffer imprisonment for conscience sake. Amen.' Over the next few months to June 1914 the Nottingham WSPU were to interrupt church services another eight or nine times. However, in June 1914 they went to their most extreme and gutted All Saints' Church in Breadsall with a large conflagration that appalled and shocked the congregation. Almost all the interior of the 13th-century church was destroyed.[9]

Unrepentant, the WSPU delivered a letter to the vicar, the Reverend Whitaker, the following day in a green envelope, which said:

'Let there be light
The price of Liberty.
Votes For Women.
The message we left
Must have been burnt.
A year ago.   A reference to Emily Wilde Davison'

However, the destruction of the church in Breadsall strained the relationship between the WSPU and local church communities around the region almost to breaking point, and when, 10 days later, they attempted to interrupt a service for the sick in St Mary's, Nottingham, they were violently thrown out and the following evening several windows in the WSPU office on Derby Road were smashed for the second time in a week.

The tolerance many church-goers had displayed over the previous 12 months had evaporated, and with it went any hopes the WSPU may have had of claiming the moral high ground. It is hard from this distance to fully understand and appreciate the damage

*Opposite: All Saints'
Church, Breadsall.*

*The interior of the church
before the fire.*

Christabel's policies had on the movement as a whole, but the experience of the women in the East Midlands serves to demonstrate that support and sympathy had all but melted away. In any propaganda war between the WSPU and the Government the women had lost the day and any repressive moves made against the WSPU were to be applauded by the general public. Throughout the country, both women and suffragette shops were attacked and damaged with little comment. Christabel had charted the WSPU on a course that would sink the cause.

The Government's reaction to the new outbreak of vandalism at the beginning of 1912, when it came in April 1913, was forceful and calculated, and within a short space of time offices of both the national headquarters of the WSPU in their new premises at Lincoln's Inn House and *The Suffragette* were raided and over 120 women were arrested. For their part, Mrs Pankhurst and the Pethick-Lawrences were arrested on charges of incitement and were consequently tried. Without doubt, this was a serious attempt by the Government to 'choke off' the national movement from its leaders, while doing their utmost to scatter and suppress the movement around the country. It was only by fate that Christabel Pankhurst was not in the office at the time and was able to escape to Paris dressed as a nurse. As Christabel Pankhurst later recalled, the arrests and the confiscation of press copy was a great blow and for a time the paper looked unable to continue, but later *The Suffragette* was

*The burnt remains of St
James's bible.*

able to continue, albeit at a reduced level. Interestingly enough, when the paper looked in danger of closing down, Ramsay MacDonald and Keir Hardie, in the interests of free speech, offered to take over the publication of *The Suffragette*. However, the offer was rejected outright by a fiercely independent Lincoln's Inn House.

In other ways, too, the increasing militancy and growing political isolation of Christabel towards the end of 1912 and the early part of 1913 had other far-reaching effects that were hard to see at the time, but in Leicester the branch undertook a new policy of recruiting working women into the movement. Clearly this course of action was a complete antithesis to what Christabel was preaching at the time and needs to be understood in the light of what was happening in London – especially the by-election in Bromley and Bow. At the end of 1912 the Labour MP, George Lansbury, resigned his seat and fought a by-election on the single issue of women's suffrage. Gripped by the possibility of a major coup should he win, the WSPU threw all their weight behind the campaign. However, the campaign was overshadowed by the accusation that the WSPU had long ceased to be concerned with the goals and ambitions of the thousands of working women living in the East End. Of course, on the face of it the union had always maintained that it sought to appeal to women of all social classes and denied the existence of any formal discrimination among its ranks.

Until this time, and despite the influence of Alice Hawkins and the Leicester branch, the WSPU had largely ignored the working class and this fundamental antagonism was on open display in the Bromley and Bow election campaign. Throughout the East End many Labour supporters, with some justification, decried the WSPU as a middle-class organisation that was only interested in a 'ladies' vote'. Chided by these accusations, the WSPU decided to undertake a programme of damage limitation and sought to dovetail the hopes and aspirations of working women into the union's political agenda. As Flora Drummond proclaimed in *The Suffragette* in November 1912:

> 'The enemies of "votes for women" are saying that the suffragette movement is a movement of rich women and women workers are taking no real part in it. The truth was that the three main objectives of the suffragette campaign were to end sweating of women workers which was undermining the health of the mothers of the race and driving thousands to a life of shame; to put a stop to the White Slave Traffic…and to prevent "the outrages committed upon little girls, some of them only babies".'

Flora Dummond, organiser of the working-class deputation to Lloyd George.

In line with this re-emphasis of the WSPU's policy, by 27 December Christabel had shifted her position somewhat and was now proclaiming that:

'The WSPU acts upon the belief that the working woman, with her more subtle mind, finer intuitions and greater knowledge of human nature, is already a more valuable citizen and more qualified for political leadership than are many male Labour leaders.'

Consequently, it was for no other reason than to answer their critics that the WSPU began to encourage membership among the working women of the East Midlands. To this end, instructions were

Newspaper cuttings of the working-class deputation.

January 24, 1913 — THE DAILY MIRROR

PICTURESQUE DEPUTATION TO THE CHANCELLOR OF THE EXCHEQUER.

sent out to all the branches to begin a recruitment drive that was to correspond with Flora Drummond's call for 300 working women to put their case before Lloyd George early in 1913.

In Leicester, of course, Alice Hawkins jumped at the chance and went to London to represent the Women's Boot and Shoe Union. She was more than eager at this time to demonstrate that the WSPU was not an organisation entirely of rich women, but that working women were also involved. With some passion, she also pointed out to Lloyd George that her two sons – one in the Navy and the other in the Army – had the vote, yet the woman who brought them into the world had no say and were 'looked down on'. In spite of the impassioned pleas by some of the women, Lloyd George would not commit himself and the deputation remained in London to prepare for any action that might follow.

In the end, the delegates achieved very little in real terms and the rejection outside the House of Commons on a wet and windy Tuesday evening heralded a period of window smashing on larger shops and Government property. At first, Flora Drummond's stance appealed directly to the working-class women within the WSPU because it allowed women to escape the role of victims and become mistresses of their own destiny within an economic context.

Consequently, the vote became a holy grail by which women could readjust their economic position within the workplace and compete with men on a more equal basis. Of course, the subordinate sexual position of women was often linked to the inferior economic position of women, and almost from its inception the WSPU's hidden agenda had been a response to the appalling poverty suffered by many women. In Leicester, this anxiety had been around for some time and had found its expression in socialism and a widespread belief that Britain was gripped not only in moral decline, but also in racial degeneration. This fear of racial degeneration was nothing new and had been around since Booth conducted his famous survey into the conditions of the London poor.

However, in Leicester 'Lydia' made much use of her column in *The Pioneer* to highlight this very problem and consistently argued that society ignored the welfare of women and children at their peril. For her, the issues were clear: the degraded economic condition of women was a terrible indictment of capitalism on working women. While men, through the activities of trade unionism, were able to improve their lot, women, by being in direct competition with men, consistently failed to benefit from protective legislation. Either they were legislated out of the workplace, or men were quick to perceive

DAILY SKETCH, FRIDAY, JANUARY 24, 1913.

'ISHERWIVES AND PIT BROW LASSES ON DEPUTATION TO CHANCELLO

(1) The Newhaven fisherwomen photographed before leaving Scotland to take part in the suffragist deputation to Mr. Lloyd George at the Treasury yesterday. (2) The fishwives, with the other working women who were on the deputation, which included factory hands from the East End of London, pit-brow lasses from Lancashire, cotton operatives from Lancashire and Yorkshire, nurses, school teachers, shop assistants

them as a rival group and make use of economic, legal and ideological weapons to eliminate or reduce their competition. Consequently, while some women and children undoubtedly benefitted from the mass of Government-sponsored social reforms that curbed the excesses of laissez-faire, men prospered more from this type of state intervention and, as a result, consistently showed little or no interest in organising women within the Labour movement.

This lack of action by male trade unionists was the nub of the problem, and while in Leicester and Northampton the long tradition of female labour in the local factories and workshops gave them a measure of independence and a relatively higher wage, they still smarted at their menfolk's inaction. However, this was not to be the case in and around Northampton after 1911. As it has already been pointed out, the men within the NUBSO actively sought to incorporate women's low pay into official union policy throughout this later period. But it was only as a direct response to the women's breakaway union in Leicester that local Boot and Shoe Union officials sought, with some success, to incorporate the local women into an organised trade union and fought for the principle of a minimum wage for all women workers. As one male leader, without a backward glance to the previous policy of the union, commented in a meeting some time later,

'By the help and the loyalty of the women, in a short time wages shall be considerably higher than they were 20 years ago.'

This commitment to women's issues is the key to understanding not only why Northampton women refused to become militant at the beginning of 1912, but also why Alice Hawkins could not export her new trade union to Northamptonshire. Of course, the situation within Northampton was not the norm, and indeed it went against much of the experience of other women around the East Midlands, but, without doubt, the new women's union in Leicester, created by Alice Hawkins and Lizzie Willson, had something to do with the unique situation of the area.

Everywhere else though, the problems of women were very real indeed, and the early radical feminists attempted to solve the problem of economic and social oppression by making their inferior position the 'problem', baulking against the male ideology that oppressed them at work and attempted to relegate them to a world of domestic chores. As a result, women of all social classes within the WSPU attacked the male concept that biological differences between the sexes were a major part in the division of labour within the industrial sphere. No longer would they accept that their 'psycho-biological metabolism' would render them a less useful member of the workforce. They now openly attacked the underlying assumption that a woman's role within the workplace was determined by her incapacity for demanding, physical work and argued that the established domestic sphere espoused by Ruskin that 'the power of women is to rule at home' only sought to hide their subservience in the means of production. Indeed, as on suffragette asked:

'What would happen if, in protest, the whole of the women workers were to return to the home and engage themselves in domestic affairs of the home? It would mean a complete dislocation of the industrial world. Therefore, for protection's sake, the women demand the franchise.'

Instead, women like Lydia in the *The Pioneer* argued, as early as 1902, that the image of the 'true woman' and the 'true family' conjured up harmony and love that often hid the true picture of violence and despair, and that any analysis of women's condition must take this into account.

Of course, Lydia was not attacking the concept of the family – that particular debate was yet to come. Instead, while insisting that the family was the cornerstone of society and therefore should be protected at all costs, the all costs did not include the subjection of women in it. As Helen Watts said in 1909:

'The love of home is one of our strongest motives of action…The sweating evil, intemperance, bad housing and many other miserable conditions in England today are among the evils with which women are called to contend for the sake of home.'

Instead, they took a more complex argument which suggested that the health of the family rested on the physical health of the wife or mother. While more often than not the home was a place of rest and recuperation for husbands and children, the home was no 'pedestal of ease' for working-class women, for, in a large majority of cases, the wife became the slave, without whose labour the whole structure of the family would collapse. As Margery Spring-Rice later maintained:

> 'Upon the survival of the mother depends the growth and care of the family, and a high rate of maternal mortality threatens in more ways than one the very existence of the race.'

Further to this, changes were being made elsewhere that only increased the isolation of the WSPU at a local level. For instance, in the north, Lancashire cotton-mill workers and the North of England Society (a constitutional suffrage organisation) had, through constant pressure at TUC and ILP conferences, succeeded in shifting the ILP towards supporting votes for women. As a result, between 1912 and 1914 the Miners' Federation reversed its long-held objections to female suffrage and threw its considerable weight into the fight. This was a major shift of policy, and in 1913 the Labour Party Conference tied itself, by a nearly two to one vote, to a motion committing members to oppose any franchise bill that excluded women.

Not only that, but this alliance was further strengthened by the announcement of the NUWSS that they would seek electoral co-operation with Labour. Under the direction of Catherine Marshall, money and skilled organisers were offered to the Labour Party to oppose anti-suffrage Liberal members at by-elections. This was a significant change in the fortunes of the suffrage campaign and the WSPU, now out of step with the wider campaign, was in a poor position to take advantage of this shift in ILP policy. It was truly ironical that, as the suffragists had slowly moved nearer to the Labour Party, so the WSPU moved away.

In Leicester, the effects of Christabel Pankhurst's policy were all too clear. From the outset of renewed militancy, members of the local Labour Party were provided with an ideal excuse to dissociate themselves from what had become an embarrassment. As Sheila Rowbotham has pointed out, men like this were obviously relieved to be let off the hook and 'remained self-righteous in the face of renewed pressure'. Indeed, MacDonald told Alice Hawkins, Mrs Iondies, Mrs Lowe, Mrs Goodliffe and Gladys Hazel, at his surgery in St Mark's Church on Belgrave Road in 1912, that theirs was an organisation that 'only spoke for a small section of women suffragists and had declared war on the Labour Party'. He had been deeply outraged by the increasing acts of arson and vandalism, and by June

1913 he wrote a leader for the *Daily Chronicle* condemning what he saw as a 'pettifogging' movement led by middle-class women, who in no way represented the minds or manners of the great mass of working women, 'whose well-being was cruelly sacrificed'.

In some ways this observation appeared quite true, for not all women trade unionists could link, as Alice Hawkins had done, the vote with the economic side of the women's question. Many trade unionists at this time argued that a mixture of the two could hinder any chances of success in Labour legislation. Thus, when MacDonald said that he welcomed the WSPU's attempts to hinder Labour, he saw this as a 'blessing' that would only lead to their removal from sensible debate 'and that is the best thing that can happen to women's suffrage'.

Clearly there was now no love lost between the two factions, and the WSPU retaliated by heckling Ramsay MacDonald in the De Montfort Hall three times in as many weeks in 1914. However, this only served to show the extent to which the WSPU had been isolated within the wider political community, and although Miss Elizabeth Grew was received with all due respect when offered an opportunity to speak at one such meeting she had all but lost the debate. Indeed, despite the fact that the WSPU were never a favourite of the *Leicester Mercury,* they came in for some sharp criticism when the newspaper wrote 'The interruptions are doing damage to the very cause they are presumably desirous of serving'. Instead, the leader continued to argue that the militancy displayed in the De Montfort Hall would never secure the franchise and would only strengthen the hands of those who contended that women's suffrage would be a blunder. In some respects, this point of view is not hard to understand.[10] Indeed, it was not only members of the Labour Left who felt disquiet at Christabel's actions, as H.W. Nevinson wrote in his journal, it is 'now going to pieces through one young woman's simple mistake'.

However, condemnation by the press fuelled more violent forms of reaction and over the next few months an arson campaign was carried out around Leicestershire with three empty mansion houses being targeted: the Red House in Burton Walk, Loughborough, on 19 October 1913, Stoughton Hall in May 1914 and Neville Holt Mansion near Market Harborough in May 1914.

However, all three attempts failed to take hold, and as a result Gladys Hazel and Margaret West applied to Lincoln's Inn House for the expertise of a professional arsonist like Kitty Marion. As Sylvia Pankhurst explained:

The burnt out waiting room at Blaby Railway Station, attacked by Leicester suffragettes.

'Certain officials of the union were given, as their main work, the task of advising incendiaries, and arranging for the supply of such inflammable materials…and other such matters as they might require.'

Kitty Marion arrived in Leicester in early June and began to instruct the branch in urban warfare with the result that, in July 1914, she, Ellen Sheriff and Elizabeth Frisby, armed with wood shavings dipped in creosol and an axe to break in, trekked across a field in the middle of the night and managed to burn down Blaby railway station, causing £500 worth of damage.

If the WSPU failed to impress the leaders of the ILP, then so too did the Labour Party fail to impress upon the Leicester WSPU that its policy of aggression would destroy any vestige of credibility it might have earned. The branch had changed too much for this type of appeal to work. By 1914 the branch was peopled by younger, radical women from the new lower middle classes, like schoolteachers and nurses. They saw their struggle for the vote in terms of a sex war against all men rather than a class conflict. It might well be argued, with some justification, that under the dictatorial leadership of Christabel Pankhurst in Paris, the campaign had become too narrow in its outlook and too divorced from local working-class politics that might have lent it the broad popular base it needed. As Rosen pointed out in *Rise Up Women*, 'The tactics of attacking empty houses and golf links was not bothersome enough to create a crisis of magnitude sufficient to bring about a passing of women's measure.'

Instead, the experience of the Leicester branch demonstrated quite clearly that it only sought to alienate those within the Labour movement who might have helped. The tactics of the revolutionary were all but lost on many local socialists who were anxious to demonstrate their respectability. Consequently, and considering the Leicester WSPU's formation owed much to its Labour origins, the Labour Party had little effect on the local leadership and could do little to prevent the outbreak of militancy in Leicester.

Almost from the declaration by Mrs Pankhurst in March 1912, the local union began to sign up volunteers to undertake what was referred to as danger duty, like Violet Doudney, a 23-year-old nurse from Stoney Stanton, who received two months hard labour in July 1912 for breaking windows in the Home Secretary's office during a WSPU demonstration.[11] In the end, the commitment to the Pankhursts was too strong, thus, when a concerted letter box attack was instigated across the country, letter boxes in Eastgates, Humberstone Road, Rutland Street and Newark Street in the town centre received attention. In this respect, it is important to point out that these attacks were not merely copycat attacks[12] but part of Christabel Pankhurst's plan of action that was to 'strike a blow at civilisation from within'. This synchronised method of attack was more fully demonstrated only a couple of months later, when one Friday night in February 1913 16 golf courses across the country were simultaneously attacked and defaced. In Leicester, the Leicester Golf Course on Stoughton Drive was targeted to great effect and, besides lighting a bonfire on the green, the message 'No Votes, No Golf' was etched into the turf. Coincidentally, one young radical, Miss Elizabeth Frisby, only lived around the corner and her father was chairman of the club.

Elsewhere the fight continued, and over the following months not only were shop windows attacked and smashed in Market Street, causing several hundred pounds worth of damage, but telephone wires were again cut in the Stoughton Road area, coincidently around the corner from Elizabeth Frisby's home. But unfortunately for the group, these actions had almost the reverse effect from that intended. Without doubt, the Leicester WSPU had greatly misread the feelings and sentiments of the local population. It never occurred to them that by attacking predominantly middle-class targets they would lose the support of working men and women. Yet that is exactly what happened; reactions to such events lost, rather than

Above: Dorothy Pethick holding a meeting in Leicester's marketplace.

Right: Sunday morning in Leicester's marketplace, a popular venue for the local WSPU.

won, support and even though it was always a risky business to hold public meetings in the marketplace, by 1913 the suffragettes had been physically assaulted on a number of occasions and their shop in Bowling Green Street sustained several broken windows.

So dangerous had public speaking become for these women that the Leicester Watch Committee requested that the WSPU refrain from further public meetings. Predictably, Alice Hawkins refused and under the watchful eye of the police continued to speak in the marketplace and hold parades around the town.

It was also suggested by the *Leicester Mercury* that the second wave of letter box attacks around the town centre in May 1913 was a direct response to Alice Hawkins and her daughter being attacked by an angry mob in the marketplace. However, the extent to which this accusation stands is now impossible to say, but some time later Alice Hawkins was arrested for damaging the Royal Mail with Brunswick Black. She pleaded guilty and was sent to prison for seven days. In her defence she claimed it was a political offence and refused to take food. But, primarily due to failing health and a request by her close family, she declined to hunger strike and was spared the indignity of being force-fed.

By 1914 the policy of using violence for a constitutional end, introduced by Christabel Pankhurst in 1912, had completely reversed all the good the WSPU had done for women's suffrage. The tactics employed by the WSPU since the departure of the Pethick-Lawrences had little effect in bringing about a Liberal reassessment of policy and had done much to destroy 'most of those WSPU members and sympathisers who possessed some intellectual independence and critical faculty of their own'. Without doubt, the arson campaign did more harm than good, and instead of recruiting sympathetic politicians and people of influence into the movement it did much to facilitate a decline in public support. Militancy had become not so much a measure forced upon them by Asquith's intransigence, but more an expression of Christabel Pankhurst's right to rule in exile. In Paris, her enforced isolation led her to believe that they were being denied the vote by a Government out of step with public opinion. Although that may have once been the case, by 1914 it was a complete delusion. Unfortunately, these feminists tended to imagine that there could be changes in a woman's position in a capitalist system without either transforming the outer world of production, the inner world of the family or their sexual status.

In many respects this was as true of Leicester as elsewhere, and the evidence suggests that having initially built an organisation with

Alice Hawkins on her way to prison after attacking pillar boxes around the town in 1913. With her is detective sergeant Ward and superintendent Caron.

a broad popular base, the Pankhursts rejected its working-class foundation and replaced it with a narrow, insular clique of middle-class women, who were, by and large, out of touch with the realities of working-class life. The WSPU's ability to limit what was, to all intents and purposes, a social revolution to one burning issue was in many people's eyes a 'great fault'. Of course, it is true to say that Alice Hawkins and a few other working-class women remained, but the policies of the national leadership had consistently cut off the WSPU from its best supporters. Instead, a majority of these women returned to the NUWSS and the WFL when a reassessment of the Labour Party's position was made clear.

However, Emmeline and Christabel Pankhurst did not think in terms of building a mass organisation or of mobilising the dissatisfaction among working women, even though women like Alice Hawkins had consistently shown them the way, and although it rendered the WSPU ineffective in Leicester and elsewhere as a viable political organisation after 1912, it did make the issue of votes for women one of burning importance in Edwardian Britain. But, there was a price to pay, 'and once they had adopted militant tactics, the choices closed in on them' as the acts of militancy appeared to take on a logic of their own. As a consequence, it was the outbreak of war in 1914 that undoubtedly prevented the further use of arson in Leicester and elsewhere. As Kitty Marion later recalled:

> 'I was on danger duty in Leicester, ready to send another reminder to the Government…when a telegram arrived from headquarters, to stop all activity.'

Almost as soon as war broke out, and without a backward glance, the Pankhursts immediately wound up all groups within the East Midlands and called their members to turn their attention to matters of war and empire.

Notes

1. There is evidence in the Fawcett Library to suggest that Christabel really wanted to burn down Nottingham Castle in the spring of 1912, as Sylvia Pankhurst later recalled a message from Christabel that read 'Would you burn down Nottingham Castle?' She replied that she would only lead a torchlight procession to the castle and fling her torch at its walls as a symbolic act.
2. Her husband was a surgeon at the Leicester Royal Infirmary.
3. According to *The Suffragette*, one was the premises of Mr Jules Richard, a camera manufacturer, valued at £15 and the other was a window valued at £60 at the premises of a jeweller, Alfred Clark.
4. Gladys Hazel controlled a wide area: Leicestershire, Nottinghamshire, Birmingham, Wolverhampton and most of the Black Country.
5. He noted in his diary in October 1913, 'The suspicions and jealousies, the reckless discharging of organisers, the refusal to have the best speakers to speak…the suspicion of the MPU, of Harben and especially of me…The whole thing is a kind of spy mania, a kind of possession. Christabel has actually thought we were plotting to extradite her! It is the nearest thing to insanity I've known in the movement.'
6. Unfortunately, nothing else is known about this woman. She is only known from this letter.
7. She wrote in *The Suffragette* on 1 August 1913 that around 75 to 80 percent of all men had been infected with venereal disease before marriage.
8. The Cat and Mouse Act, or the Prisoners Temporary Discharge for Ill Heath Act, 1913, authorised the release of prisoners who had become ill due to hunger striking. However, once better, they were subject to rearrest.
9. According to documents held at the church, it is believed that the fire was started by Alice Wheeldon, aged 47, and her daughter Hetty Wheeldon, who both later confessed after the campaign was wound up. However, there is also circumstantial evidence that they were assisted by Irene Casey. According to the *Nottingham Daily Express* (3 July 1914), when she was arrested in Nottingham a month later police found in her possession a 20ft fuse, a detonator, 5lbs of cheddite, two fire lighters, a small bottle of benzine, two boxes of matches, a glass cutter, a pair of pliers and a book on Nottingham churches, including one relating to Breadsall. There is also an interesting footnote pertaining to Alice Wheeldon. In 1917 both she and her daughter Hetty Wheeldon were arrested and charged with attempting to assassinate the Prime Minister, Lloyd George.
10. According to *The Suffragette* (20 March 1914), one action that enraged local ILP members was the unveiling of a socialist flag, stained with black ink, with the shout 'Your flag is stained with dishonour'. This so enraged the men that the meeting was suspended for 15 minutes while the women were ejected.
11. She told the magistrate, 'I broke the window as a protest against the inhuman treatment of suffragist prisoners, and to take my part in the agitation. I am not sorry, on the contrary, as an English woman I am proud to stand here today.' *Leicester Chronicle*, 6 July 1912.
12. This was not entirely true. In both Nottingham and Leicester there were copycat attacks on pillar boxes by impressionable youngsters. In Leicester, Charles Garrets, a boot boy from the George Hotel, ruined letters in East Gates and the High Street. He claimed in court that he got the idea from a suffragette meeting he had attended. In Nottingham, on the other hand, in October 1912 a 16-year-old girl, Beatrice Jarman of Stanley Street, Newark, was bound over for 12 months for attempting to set fire to a letterbox on the corner of her street. She claimed she was a suffragette.

Conclusion:
Themes and Issues within the WSPU

'Ideas travel upwards, manners downwards.'
Bulwer

In contrast to the national movement, the Leicester WSPU, a constituent mix of WSPU activists and a curious assortment of political idealists and hard-headed trade unionists, ostensibly ran from 1907 to 1914, and during this time they underwent considerable transformations; theirs and Alice Hawkins's story is one of change and development initiated through the policies of one woman, Christabel Pankhurst. In some respects, this is the key to unravelling the often confusing and contradictory chain of events that occurred during this period. Officious and omnipotent, she cast her long shadow over the movement with a power and personal influence that was to shape and mould the organisation in her own image.

Consequently, an investigation into the life of Alice Hawkins would not have been possible without reference to the wider movement, with its contrived and centrally-directed policies, indeed, it is a salient point never to underestimate the significance of political and sociological influences in formulating a movement and its ideology.

Thus, when investigating women like Alice Hawkins, it is not always easy to understand their motivations and ambitions, for, to each, the ideas and beliefs were as varied as they were many; as with all struggles for equality and justice, the movement touched and involved women from all classes within society. The Leicester WSPU were, by and large, an alliance of Liberals, Socialists, Nonconformists, Evangelicals and Primrose Leaguers, but for the duration and for the cause they joined together under the feminist banner of militant suffragists to seek a conclusion to the reform that had begun in the 1860s. At first, the differences of opinion that existed between the members of the alliance seemed trivial, but in reality the calm coexistence hid a wealth of hostility, misunderstanding and concern and, despite the fact that it can be argued that their aims were much the same, their motives were not.

Indeed, in some respects it is possible to argue that the form which the WSPU took after 1910 only satisfied the passions and ambitions of a younger, middle-class activist, and although they were finally to put the Leicester branch, at least, on a more professional footing their efforts made them vulnerable to the charge that they had all but abandoned the working class for a privileged vote. Even despite their later attempts to win working-class support by attacking the unequal power between men and women within the workplace, the WSPU became increasingly isolated, not only from the lively political debate that was taking place within the town halls and meeting halls in boroughs the length and breadth of the country, but also from the Labour Left.

And nowhere is this more important than when it is remembered that the formation of the Leicester WSPU was intrinsically bound up in Labour politics and the women's trade union movement. Alice Hawkins and others had, to their credit, not only been deeply involved in the birth of the Leicester Labour Party, but also the Labour clubs attached to it, like the Clarion Cycle Club. This club, with its emphasis on the bicycle, was a potent force throughout the 1890s, not only as an engine of liberation, but also as a vehicle for socialist ideals and a shaper of Labour opinion.

The bicycle was often seen as an engine of liberation for many women.

It was unique in its day and, although the Clarion vans carried their message far and wide, its socialism was something the average working man and woman could understand. Consequently, it was through the pages of its official organ, *The Clarion*, that many Leicester women were introduced to Christabel Pankhurst's views on women's suffrage in 1904 and 1905. Christabel Pankhurst had made much use of *The Clarion's* popular appeal to working women to publicise the infant WSPU's policies, and when she approached Leicester's trades council's executive committee to come and speak to its members, she was accepted without delay and arrived in Leicester on 18 July 1905.

The acceptance of WSPU speakers on Labour and socialist platforms was entirely in keeping with Labour thought and policy. Indeed, many leading members within the Labour movement, like Keir Hardie, saw the two groups as part of the same movement.

The New Woman.

HAVE DINNER READY AT ONE O'CLOCK, JOHN!

272

As a result, it seemed to the women of Leicester only a natural extension of Labour policy to involve themselves in such matters, but because of Christabel's policies towards the ILP, the honeymoon was not to last and tensions between the women and the ILP destroyed all vestige of support and co-operation. Indeed, Christabel was determined to work independently of other organisations and political parties, even if this meant not only jeopardising nearly 10 years of patient trade union effort, but also abandoning every political objective for the sake of just one issue.

Yet that did not mean to say that women like Alice Hawkins would immediately forsake issues of Labour, far from it, but as a result the road to the formation of the Leicester branch of the WSPU was built on the horns of a dilemma. On the one hand, as committed socialists and members of both the ILP and the Women's Co-op Guild, their loyalties naturally inclined towards the Labour Party. However, to Alice Hawkins and the other women, there appeared to be little choice, and they quite happily ditched their male colleagues for the sake of just one issue – votes for women.

Moreover, the policies of Christabel Pankhurst were to have a profound effect on a branch such as Leicester; the political theory developed from the pen of Christabel Pankhurst appeared to have little in common with the average working woman within the town. This was because a contradiction appeared that was both confusing and counterproductive. While proclaiming that women who were already in the WSPU knew no barriers of class distinction, the reality at grass-roots level was very different. The elitism increasingly displayed by individual members had an off-putting effect on women who were still ideologically Socialist. Not only were the tactics and policies of the WSPU alienating large sections of the working class across the Midlands, but on a national level the organisation itself was becoming detached from its Labour origins.

Paradoxically, and despite Christabel's opinions on working women in the WSPU, there appeared to be a real concern within the London headquarters at this steady desertion from the Leicester branch, and by 1911 Sylvia Pankhurst, at the behest of Dorothy Pethick, appealed directly to working-class women through the pages of *The Pioneer* by writing a series of articles on the problems of working women and their grievances under the new Insurance Act. Further, the national leadership undertook a series of meetings around Leicester to promote the WSPU as a party that was concerned with working-class problems.

For example, in April 1912 Mrs Flora Drummond and Georgina Brackenbury attended a meeting in the Corn Exchange where they addressed the concerns and worries of working women. Indeed, in an attempt at solidarity with many of the women sitting in the stalls, Mrs Drummond said that, having joined the ILP over 10 years before, she was still 'interested in the industrial question and inequality of women in the workplace'. Unfortunately, it is hard to say exactly how successful these attempts were, but by August 1913, much to the delight of Alice Hawkins, the Leicester WSPU began a concerted effort to recruit women from both the trade union movement and the ILP by addressing them directly through their meetings as part of their autumn campaign.

Yet despite the fact that the number of women joining trade unions was rising in real terms, they were fighting a losing battle for the hearts and minds of Leicester's working women. Not only were a majority of these women alienated by acts of militancy on private property, they also rejected the WSPU's policy of a limited franchise as foolish. This loss of support was recognised by Mrs Billington-Greig when she argued that the WSPU, in its earliest days, could rely on working-class support, but extreme militancy had since weakened its mass support.

By 1912–13 the branch, with the exception of its small working-class core, had, in effect, moved too far to the Right to have much in common with the realities of factory life. Still, that is not to say that all working-class women felt the same way and, although the numbers were relatively small, some new recruits filtered into the branch at various times between 1912–14, notably Ellen Sheriff, niece of the Labour radical Amos Sheriff and a Young Hot Blood from the boot and shoe trade, who arguably became the branch's most successful arsonist under the supervision of Kitty Marion.

Without doubt, this was primarily due to the input and influence of women like Alice Hawkins, Bertha Clark and Mrs Lowe. Although badly mauled in the process of embourgeoisement, the WSPU in Leicester could never completely ditch its working-class origins, nor indeed did it really want to, and over the years appeals often went out to these women to come and support them in their fight. Indeed, as Mrs Fagin confirmed in a trades council debate on the Conciliation Bill in 1911, 'there were a considerable number of working women in the WSPU' doing good work on behalf of working women. As such, throughout this later period these women, with their good sense and hopes of social harmony, quietly inspired and led the younger and more impressionable Edwardian schoolteacher.

Of course, Alice Hawkins and Bertha Clark were of a different temperament from the Young Hot Bloods who later peopled the group after 1910. They had been schooled in the politics of agitation at the cutting edge of industrial conflict, where open-air meetings were woven into the very fabric of working-class life. Consequently, the contrasting image of the working-class suffragette against the more popular London model was a familiar sight to the crowds gathered in the marketplace to hear the latest polemic between the Government and the WSPU. Their concerns and worries, therefore, were never completely marginalised and when national leaders attended meetings within the town, they tempered their message to suit their audience and spoke in terms of women's low wages and poor working conditions.

But, in reality, working women within the boot and shoe industry, who might have been tempted to join the group, felt alienated in a movement that had become blatantly middle class under the direction of Dorothy Pethick. From 1911 onwards, the Leicester branch encountered little enthusiasm for their policies at factory gates among female shoe operatives within the town and often appealed to this group for more support. Indeed, the older members who were already involved in the formation of the branch had, with the exception of a few hardcore supporters of the Pankhurst family, begun to feel marginalised within their own organisation by the influx of young middle-class women.

Yet, for her part, Alice Hawkins could distinguish between Labour politics and the work done by the WSPU. While championing the rights of working women within the trade union movement, she understood only too well that the Pankhursts' WSPU represented the best chance women had of achieving the vote, however limited. For her, what was more important was that a breach be made in male intransigence. Once this breakthrough had been made, history would be on their side and an enfranchisement of working women would be sure to follow. By 1912 there were many within the WSPU who believed that the country was suffering from two evils, the subjection of labour and the subjection of women. By eliminating the political subjection of women, other reforms were sure to follow. But, as many women understood only too well, this type of approach to the problem was impractical and impossible, and any attempt to canvass for full female suffrage would have to wait until men had universal suffrage. Therefore, because they were fighting for political, social and economic equality as it then stood, they argued that women should only have the vote on the same terms as men, which led them to being accused of only seeking votes for ladies.

As the Leicester branch progressed under the domination of Dorothy Pethick and its working-class heritage was seen to fade, the authority and prestige of Alice Hawkins remained an important ideological factor. She remained obligated and committed to the Pankhurst family and when the leadership of the WSPU all but abandoned its working-class origins, these strong local women refused to abandon their leaders. The reasons for this persistent loyalty are, as yet, unclear, but the admiration of some of these women bordered on the sycophantic. Indeed, Alice Hawkins often referred to Mrs Pankhurst as 'our beloved leader'. Nevertheless, at no time throughout this period did one charismatic leader arise from

Two postcards from Alice Hawkins's scrapbook.

the ranks of either the trade union movement or the Labour Party in Leicester to take control and direct grass-roots radicalism on either feminist or socialist policies.

Both Mr T. Richardson, president of the local boot and shoe trade union, and Ramsay MacDonald refused to give the lead these women needed. Indeed, not by any stretch of the imagination was MacDonald a radical in the vein of Tom Mann, and he consistently refused to stick his neck out on contentious policies. Conversely, Tom Mann made much headway with women like Alice Hawkins with his pamphlet *Leisure For Working Wives,* published in June 1890. In this document Mann proposed that women, faced with the insalubrious rounds of washing, cooking and cleaning for husbands and children, should organise collective co-operative child care and domestic duties. This type of thinking not only appealed to their socialist and co-operative backgrounds, but as Tom Mann shifted further to the Left some of the Leicester women went with him.

Given the reluctance of many of their male colleagues to support the WSPU, it is probable that Alice Hawkins and, to a lesser extent, Bertha Clark took a more pragmatic approach to the question of votes for women. While other working women appeared to feel compromised by Christabel's hostile policies towards the ILP, Alice argued that to disassociate herself from the WSPU would mean rejecting the only realistic method of achieving the vote. It must be remembered that these women had been much affected by the Employer's Federation counter-attacks on trade unionism and the lowering of wages within the boot and shoe industry. Consequently, they had been attracted to an organisation that, at first glance, seemed to offer more than just hope at some later date. Indeed, up until 1906 the non-militant organisations within the town had consistently failed to attract these radical women.

Thus, what the WSPU could offer, despite the increasing use of violence and arson in later years, was a realistic campaign that directly related to their independence and militant backgrounds. This was simply a local factor; Leicester always had a strong number of working women who were, to some extent, economically independent. This allegiance to the WSPU was certainly true in the case of Alice Hawkins and some of the other women working in the Equity Boot and Shoe Co-operative factory. They only too readily abandoned the ILP in favour of a women's political party that would deal with industrial and economic issues as they saw them.

On a wider point, it is also important to understand the economic conditions within the town, for it would seem that economic prosperity had much to do with militant development. However, evidence other than the indicator of addresses within the town was extremely sparse, and so there was a reliance on the area in which a member lived to gauge wealth and influence. For example, women like Mrs Swain and her daughters who lived on Regents Road in Leicester were clearly not working class, nor, judging by the size of the house, lower middle class. But, more importantly, we know who these women were, or at least the shakers and movers within the organisation.

These women honestly believed that once women had gained the vote they could rid the world of its wars, poverty and other social evils and, once middle-class women had the vote, they would have a duty to ensure any future legislation prevented the sexual and economic exploitation of working-class women. Indeed, the concern of some middle-class women for the rights of lower-class women was indeed a genuine one, although perhaps not always an active one.

Consequently, both sides of the social strata believed they were laying the way for future generations and that the vote was an enabling issue, or a hub around which the spokes of many feminist issues could be attached.

Clearly these were missed opportunities for an organisation that professed to being interested in all aspects of women's lives. Of course, working-class women joined but their grievances were never fully addressed or understood, nor were issues of class addressed in a positive way. For many working-class women, oppression not only existed in their lack of a political voice but also subjection within the workplace and even the home were far more important, for the simple fact that they had to deal with these issues on a daily basis.

These issues were too immediate to be ignored for a metaphysical dream, laced around an ideology that would not pay the bills or meet the rent. What relevance would Christabel's words have in the back-to-back yards beneath the shadow of the shoe and hosiery factory? For these women, domestic labour was not only unpaid, but it was undervalued and a 'real problem'. Thus, while the vote appeared to be a lofty ideal, unrelated to everyday struggles of hunger and poverty, the decision to restrict the WSPU to just one issue isolated many women because it could not distinguish between the personal and the political, and between the family and the wider economy.

Thus, for thousands of women the realities of the home, poverty and the endless routine of childcare were more important than campaigning, shoulder to shoulder, for the vote with women who had no perception of the realities of their lives. In the end, and despite Alice Hawkins's bold attempts, the WSPU in Leicester could not, or would not, provide the basis on which a broader women's movement could be based. Instead, many women would remain invisible to the movement because, not only were they of little or no economic importance, they were also isolated within the home. Unlike many working-class women at work in the factories and shops, their isolation proved a greater barrier to the organisation than oppression within the workplace. In other ways, too, the direction and motivation of the WSPU proved restricting for many women. The reluctance of Christabel Pankhurst to officially align or amalgamate the WSPU with the female trade union movement debarred many working women from joining the organisation and restricted the movement to a small band of dedicated followers.

Again, this refusal to get involved with women's issues denied many women the self-confidence to take control of their own lives. Instead, the low economic status of women's work combined to make the female workforce highly vulnerable to 'deferential pressure'. Not surprisingly then, and despite the publicity-motivated attempts to recruit working women into the organisation, there is little evidence to suggest that the WSPU made any real impact on working-class women.

In this sense, possibly due to their political heritage, many working women sought equality on men's terms, and most certainly did not set out to change society in any revolutionary way. Therefore, it is unlikely that a common goal was either perceived or desired. Of

Two postcards from Alice Hawkins's scrapbook.

MRS. BAINES.

National Women's Social and Political Union, 4, Clements Inn, W.C.

VOTES FOR WOMEN.

Miss HELEN FRASER,

Organiser, Women's Social and Political Union, 4, Clement's Inn, Strand, W.C.

course, the vote was a common goal, but in reality different perceptions lay behind the campaign for the vote and what women could achieve with the vote. On this level, each woman believed her life was therefore a process of change and that their lives were, in themselves, a revolution. However bold and romantic this movement might now seem, in reality it evolved from a sequence of events that could well have led elsewhere. Even without the benefit of hindsight and an almost heavenly faith in their cause, women on both sides of the social divide had no real way of telling that their efforts would in fact lead to a critical process of change that would bring with it votes for women. Yet that is not to forget how radical the original dream of getting the vote was.

Many women understood only too well that they were attempting to frame a world that challenged all the current perceptions of what women should be. Thus, like true revolutionaries, they explored every possible means of persuasion and debate, and when that failed they resorted to arson, vandalism and acts of violence against members of the Government, and, for some, the prospect of militant action was all important, and many answered the Pankhursts' call with delight and enthusiasm.

Of course, there was a downside and many local WSPU members were physically attacked in the street, facing wrath and ostracism from their own communities. However, the brutality meted out to suffragettes went much deeper than the rough and tumble nature of Edwardian politics. The savagery directed towards the WSPU and non-militant organisations before World War One differed from the type of mass violence which greets all unfamiliar movements in their early stages. Instead, violence against women suffragettes was not only prompted by a deeper social concern regarding the role of women within the family, but it also had a direct correlation with militant tactics after 1912. Indeed, this connection was all the more strengthened by the refusal of the Government to accept the legitimacy of the suffragettes' claim for votes for women.

As a result, male aggression had deeper roots than merely the need for revenge at the destruction of private property. Within these acts of violence lay a more profound and disquieting motive, and contrary to the belief that 'industrial society had cured men of their aggression', many men were more than willing to show their objections towards votes for women for purely personal reasons other than those enshrined in politics. Now, their anger was sharply focused on the changing role of women within the home. For many men there was an inherent risk that politically active women would endanger the future of the family itself. It was argued with some passion that if women were doing their duty within the household then they would have little time for politics. By definition, political activity could only mean that a woman was neglecting her family and household duties and this in turn would inevitably lead to the break up of the family.

Instead, they held to the traditional custom that, upon marriage, a woman takes on the politics of her husband and any attempts by individuals or organisations to challenge this view was perceived as a threat to their position within the family. While many men were imbued with Victorian aristocratic values of chivalry and sought to protect their womenfolk from the hardships of political life, many working-class men, unable to vocalise their feelings, were more than willing to resort to violence to protect their social standing. Nor was this violence confined to the home; innocent women were sometimes attacked in the street if they were suspected of being a suffragette. In Leicester, young suffragettes were attacked outside the Old White Swan public house in the marketplace and their stall of sweets and cakes was burnt by disgruntled males.

In some respects, militancy within their own areas was a braver action than that committed by women within the capital. Up to a point, the London women were anonymous and could lose themselves in a sea of faces. But in Leicester, we see the communities smaller and the infamy greater. These women could be, and indeed were, identified and offered up to public ridicule by their own neighbours. Indeed, fear of being seen as unusual or out of step with public opinion was a serious impediment to social and political action, especially to women. But by transferring their allegiance and loyalty to a feminist group that had a measure and purpose about it, they were, like Alice Hawkins, able to transcend this compelling need to avoid moral and social isolation.

In many ways Alice Hawkins was a confusing paradox. As a committed socialist and ILP member she remained dedicated and obligated to the Pankhurst dogma and an undemocratic organisation. But, in the end, Alice Hawkins provided a role model that proved, beyond doubt, women's capabilities in political affairs. The issues of privilege and wealth, so easily abandoned by the middle-class members, were a major concern to her, and after the campaign was wound up in 1914 she returned to the ranks of the Labour Party where she spent the rest of her life dedicating herself to the service of others. At no time was she an easy woman to deal with, as her descendants have testified, but her strong sense of duty and social justice made her, in many ways, an uncompromising woman, and she was still promoting Labour issues around the streets of Leicester a week before she died at the ripe old age of 83.

So what we see within this woman is a profile of a suffragette who was both good and bad. Here was a woman who existed by virtue of imprisonment and the hunger strike, who embarked on a path that, ultimately, isolated wider support for the cause but who would stand firm and proud in what one Nottingham suffragette once termed as the 'shrieking sisterhood'.

Appendices

H. M. Prison
Holloway
London
22nd February 1907

Dear Mr MacDonald,

I received your letter this morning by special permission of the governor. I was pleased to hear from you, but sorry to see the stand you take over the enfranchisement of women for I quite thought you were in favour of it. But I see I was mistaken. You say the Women's Social and Political Union stirred up trouble interest up to a certain point (sic). Well if we had abandoned at that point we might as well never began. For it is only by bringing constantly before the public notice our wrongs that anything will ever be done. For you known how quickly the public can forget and we are determined to bring Englishmen to a sense of their duty to women. For the time as passed to put her to one side.

Now, as for the ILP voting against the enfranchisement of women. I hope not, for if they do, I am afraid they will lose a great deal number of members and just now I would think they are quite afraid to do that, (because) as I understand the ILP programme, that is one of their chief (aims). The constitution of the ILP, the equality of the sexes, is one of the chief items in it. So I sincerely hope they will not go back on their pledge.

Now Mr MacDonald, you ask if there is anything I want done. I thank you, but there is nothing just now, as I shall finish my sentence of fourteen days which (expires ?) on Wednesday 27th. But I should like the Home Secretary, if it were possible, told that, Woman thinks him a coward for ordering mounted police out to ride down women who would have come peaceable enough to see them, if they would allow them. No other civilized country would treat women in such a manner. But it seems he is only another Asquith. And we only have to remember Featherstone and other places to know what to expect from such men. But it makes we women think they are a little bit afraid of us.

But as we know, someone had to suffer for every reform that has ever been granted. I shall not grumble at what I have suffered if it only helps in ever so little towards the goals we are working for. Why, even our old friend Tom Mann is suffering now in the same way over the (years ?) for future (political ?) freedom suffered (some?) years ago in England. I wonder if you men think they have done wrong. You know it was the only way to get what we want.

With kind regards to your wife and self. A sister for freedom.

Alice Hawkins. Leicester.

Chronology of Events Within The East Midlands 1907–14

1907

17 January	Leicester trades council accepted WSPU speakers, Annie Kenney, Mrs Billington-Greig and Mrs Cobden-Saunders to talk at meeting.
11 February	Margaret MacDonald and other members of the Leicester NUWSS attended the 'Mud March' in London.
13 February	Leicester women took part in the demonstrations at Westminster. Alice Hawkins was arrested and sent to prison for seven days.
19 March	Christabel Pankhurst, Mrs Rothwell and Alice Hawkins spoke at the Shoe Trade Hall in Leicester to talk about their prison experiences.
21 March	Alice Hawkins announced that the Leicester branch of the WSPU had been set up.
9 April	Inaugural meeting of the Leicester WSPU branch was held in the Welford Coffee House; Mrs Barnes presided.
10 April	Miss Edith Gittins of the Leicester NUWSS spoke at a Women's Labour League meeting. She divorced herself from the tactics of Alice Hawkins in London.
15 April	First official meeting of the Leicester WSPU was held in the Welford Coffee House.
28 May	Emmeline Pankhurst, Sylvia Pankhurst and Mary Gawthorpe arrived in Oakham, Leicestershire, to oppose the Liberal candidate.
31 May	After the Rutland by-election, both Sylvia Pankhurst and Mary Gawthorpe moved to Leicester to assist in the running of the branch.
6 June	First open-air meeting held by the Leicester WSPU in the market square. Mary Gawthorpe spoke.
14 July	Sylvia Pankhurst and Alice Hawkins spoke in Leicester marketplace.
16 July	Sylvia Pankhurst and Alice Hawkins spoke in Northampton marketplace.
27 July	Sylvia Pankhurst spoke at a meeting in Harvey Lane Adult School, Leicester.
September	Mrs Despard, Teresa Billington-Greig and Edith How-Martyn leave the WSPU and form the Women's Freedom League.
14 September	The Leicester branch of the NUWSS took the right to vote to the Revisiting Barrister's Court. The court rejected their claim.
October	*Votes For Women* was first published.
16 October	The WSPU began a campaign in Nottingham. Both Christabel Pankhurst and Mrs Baldock held meetings around the town and county.
26 October	Evelyn Carryer stood as an Independent, against the Labour candidate, in Leicester's Municipal Elections for the Wycliffe Ward. She lost.
27 November	Mansfield NUWSS reject militant methods.
28 November	Christabel Pankhurst is barred from addressing students at Nottingham's University College.
28 November	Nottingham's University College reverses its decision. Several Governors resigned.
28 November	Nottingham University College students arrange for Christabel Pankhurst to speak in Woodborough Road Baptist Schoolrooms.
December	Nellie Kenney is appointed to run the Nottingham WSPU. It was a 12-month appointment.
2 December	Christabel Pankhurst and Mrs Pethick-Lawrence attempted to hold a meeting in Nottingham's Mechanics' Hall, but it was broken up by university students.
9 December	The WSPU held a second, women-only meeting in Nottingham's Circus Street Hall. Christabel Pankhurst and Miss Lamb spoke.

11 December	The WSPU attempted to disrupt Asquith's meeting in Nottingham's Mechanics' Hall. Four women were ejected from the meeting.
13 December	The WSPU attempted to disrupt Mr Harcourt's meeting at Radcliffe-On-Trent. The women were attacked and nearly thrown in the river.

1908

11 January	Leicester WSPU held a meeting at the Welford Coffee House. Evelyn Carryer and Bertha Clark sent an official protest to the Town's Council for their refusal to appoint a female Probation Officer.
21 January	Leicester WSPU held a meeting in the Welford Coffee House. Mrs Pethick-Lawrence spoke. She was invited by Evelyn Carryer and Alice Hawkins.
22 January	The Labour Party rejected WSPU claims and declined to support votes for women on their terms.
11/13 February	Both Leicester and Nottingham WSPU branches attended Women's Parliament in Caxton Hall in London.
8 March	The Leicester WSPU, Women's Liberal Association and the NUWSS organised a large Suffrage Sunday meeting in the Temperance Hall Ramsay MacDonald, Mr Grayson and Mr Snowden attended.
18 March	Nottingham WSPU held their first public meeting in the Mechanics' Hall, Nottingham. Miss Barrett from London spoke.
21 March	10,000 women, including delegations from Nottingham and Leicester, attended the Albert Hall meeting in London.
11 April	Nottingham WSPU held a meeting in Victoria Station Hotel. Over 450 ladies attended to hear Christabel Pankhurst speak.
7 May	Emmeline Pankhurst and Miss Brackenbury paid a flying visit to Nottingham. They held a meeting in the Mechanics' Hall.
9 May	Isobel Logan, daughter of the Market Harborough MP Paddy Logan, resigned from the Women's Liberal Association and joined the Leicester WSPU.
17 May	Alice Hawkins began a campaign to try and recruit working women into the WSPU from the Leicestershire village of Enderby.
30 May	A large demonstration was held in London. Although, largely a NUWSS march, many Leicester women attend, including Evelyn Carryer and Isobel Logan.
13 June	Alice Hawkins and Nellie Kenney conducted a week's campaign in Leicester and Loughborough. They attempted to raise funds to allow working women to attend the demonstration in London.
15 June	Lizzie Willson complained to a Boot and Shoe Union meeting in Higham Ferris that not enough was being done to help female workers.
21 June	Massive Hyde Park demonstration. Both Leicester and Nottingham sent members and Alice Hawkins spoke at one of the several meetings taking place. Purple, white and green were adopted as the official colours of the WSPU.
30 June	A large WSPU demonstration to Parliament. The police turned them back, and two women broke windows in 10 Downing Street as a protest. Isobel Logan, from Leicester, was arrested and sent to prison.
1 July	Nottingham WSPU held a meeting in Long Eaton marketplace. Nellie Kenney spoke.
Mid July	Miss Gladice Keevil was appointed regional organiser for the East Midlands, with responsibility of both the Leicester and Nottingham branches.
18 July	Alice Hawkins and Nellie Kenney spoke in Nottingham marketplace.
20 July	Large WSPU meeting in Nottingham, 'On the Forest'. 30,000 people attended and heard Mrs Pankhurst, Alice Hawkins, Nellie Kenney and others speak.
25 July	Alice Hawkins and Lizzie Willson held a meeting in Leicester's marketplace to try and encourage more women to join the Union and the suffragettes.

27 July	Gladice Keevil and Alice Hawkins held a large meeting in Leicester's marketplace.
1 August	Gladice Keevil and Nellie Kenney spent two weeks in Leicestershire and Nottinghamshire speaking at open-air meetings, with some success.
8 August	Leicester WSPU member, Isobel Logan, invited Clarion Cycle Club to a tea at her father's house in East Langton.
16 August	While on holiday in Tenby, Leicester WSPU member Isobel Logan held meetings around the town.
29 August	Both Lizzie Willson and Alice Hawkins held meetings around Leicester to try and recruit women into the trade union movement.
17 September	Alice Hawkins and Gladice Keevil held a meeting for working women in the lecture hall, at the request of United Trades Club in Kettering.
October	Start of an organised campaign of harassing Cabinet Ministers.
3 October	Leicester WSPU member, Isobel Logan attended a local NUWSS meeting. She championed the militant cause.
11 October	The WSPU staged a demonstration in Trafalgar Square. Several Leicester women, including Eva Lines, attended.
12 November	Sylvia Pankhurst attended a WSPU meeting in the Mechanics' Hall, Nottingham.
16 November	Christabel Pankhurst and Evelyn Carryer from Leicester held a WSPU meeting in the Boot and Shoe Trade Hall.
18 November	Leicester WSPU attempted to disrupt Asquith's meeting in Nuneaton.
December	Nellie Kenney retired as organiser for the Nottingham WSPU.
12 December	Mr Birrell is accosted in Nottingham by the local WSPU. The branch organised a second meeting in Trinity Square, Nottingham. Sylvia Pankhurst and Charlotte Marsh spoke.

1909

10 January	In Leicester, Edith New spoke in the marketplace for two hours.
14 January	Anti's held a meeting in Nottingham's Mechanics' Hall. Charles Dickens's granddaughter, Mary Angela, told them that a woman's vote was 'irresponsible'.
15 January	Winston Churchill heckled by Leicester's WSPU members.
24 January	Leicester WSPU's meeting attacked in marketplace.
25 January	Emmeline Pankhurst spoke at the Corn Exchange in Leicester. Earlier in the day, Mrs Bennett held an 'At Home' in the Wyvan Hotel.
25 January	Gladice Keevil addressed a WSPU meeting at the Mechanics' Hall, Nottingham.
30 January	Gladice Keevil and a selection of Nottingham WSPU members were arrested for obstruction outside Winston Churchill's meeting at the Victoria Hall, Nottingham.
24 February	Women's deputation to Parliament. Helen Watts from Nottingham was arrested and gaoled.
10 March	A Nottingham WSPU member addressed a meeting of the Nottingham Scottish Association to plead the militant cause.
25 March	Helen Watts returned to Nottingham to receive a hero's welcome.
26 March	Emmeline Pankhurst attended a WSPU meeting in the Mechanics' Hall, Nottingham.
27 March	The WSPU announced that they now had eleven branches nationwide.
4 April	A woman was attacked in Nottingham. She was suspected of being a suffragette.
6 April	Nottingham's Women's Liberal Association refused a request from the local WSPU to support women's suffrage.
10 April	Selina Cooper addressed a joint meeting of both the NUWSS and WSPU in St Marks' schoolrooms in Leicester.
13/26 May	Women's Exhibition at the Prince's Skating Rink in Knightsbridge. Helen Watts, from Nottingham and Alice Hawkins from Leicester held a joint stall.

22 June	Miss Helen Ogston spoke at a WSPU meeting in Nottingham's marketplace.
23 June	Nottingham WSPU held a Garden Party at 5 Mapperley Road, Nottingham. Miss Helen Ogston spoke.
29 June	Deputation to Parliament. Windows were broken in Whitehall, Downing Street and the Treasury Offices. Dorothy Pethick, Dorothy Bowker and Isobel Logan, from Leicester, and Miss Rawson and Nellie Crocker from Nottingham, were arrested and sent to gaol.
1 July	Miss Burgess resigned as secretary to the Nottingham WSPU.
1 July	Gladice Keevil told the Nottingham branch that because they had a membership of 350, Nellie Crocker was soon to be appointed as paid organiser.
5 July	Marion Wallace Dunlop was the first to adopt the hunger strike as a protest.
13 / 14 July	Stone-throwers in Holloway adopted the hunger strike. They were released.
Mid July	Nellie Crocker was appointed to run the Nottingham WSPU. She was later joined by Gladys Roberts, to act as her assistant.
13 July	Nellie Crocker addressed a meeting in Nottingham's marketplace.
25 July	Nottingham WSPU opened a shop and office at Carlton Street, Nottingham.
27 July	Nottingham WSPU attempted to disrupt Sir James Yoxall's meeting in the Albert Hall, Nottingham. Ejected from the meeting, they held a large meeting in the marketplace. Helen Watts, Charlotte Marsh, Laura Ainsworth and Mrs Baines were arrested and released without charge.
4 September	Both Alice Hawkins of Leicester and Helen Watts from Nottingham were gaoled for disrupting Winston Churchill's meeting in the Palace Theatre.
6 September	The Nottingham WSPU held a protest meeting in the marketplace to object to the arrests of WSPU members in Leicester.
8 September	Alice Hawkins, Helen Watts and the other women were released from Leicester Prison.
13 September	Helen Watts arrived back in Nottingham. She had been unfit to travel after her hunger strike. Miss Rawson was expected to arrive some days later. She was still too ill.
24 September	The start of force-feeding on Laura Ainsworth in Birmingham caused a public outrage.
October	Laura Ainsworth was appointed to run the Leicester WSPU.
7 October	Miss Helen Ogston spoke at a Social Reform League meeting at the Circus Street Hall, Nottingham.
8 October	Miss Helen Ogston launched the Nottingham Autumn campaign with an 'At Home'; she announced that a number of national leaders would visit the town over the coming months.
9 October	Nottingham WSPU held a meeting at the Mechanics' Hall. Dr Fairfield presided and Gladys Roberts and Nellie Crocker spoke.
12 October	Miss Douglas-Smith and Miss Brackenbury addressed the WSPU meeting in the Victoria Hall, Leicester.
28 October	Nellie Crocker addressed a WSPU meeting in the Circus Street Hall, Nottingham.
12 November	Lady Isabel Margerson addressed a WSPU meeting in Nottingham's Morley's Café.
18 November	Nellie Crocker held a WSPU meeting at the Church School Rooms, Beeston, while Mrs Pethick-Lawrence spoke at a meeting in Ilkeston.
20 November	Christabel Pankhurst and regional organiser Gladice Keevil attempted to hold a meeting at the Derby Drill Hall. The meeting was disrupted.
22 November	Lady Constance Lytton and Miss Brackenbury addressed a WSPU meeting at the Temperance Hall in Leicester.
23 November	The Hon Mrs Haverfield addressed a WSPU meeting at Nottingham's Morley's Café. The branch announced its coming campaign in the towns and villages of Nottinghamshire.

6 December	Leicester nurse J. Elsie Roe-Brown was arrested for breaking Post Office windows in Edinburgh and sent to prison for 15 days.
11 December	The Nottingham WSPU held a meeting in the Circus Street Hall. They announced their plans for the January General Election. Dorothy Pethick, on her way to Leicester from Newcastle, spoke.
17 December	Dorothy Pethick and Dorothy Bowker arrived in Leicester to take over as organisers for the branch. They lived at 11 Severn Street.

1910

4 January	The London WSPU held a meeting in Northampton marketplace. Police prevented the meeting from being broken up.
8 January	Elsa Gaye, from the Leicester WSPU, helped the Loughborough branch in their General Election campaign.
8 January	The Leicester WSPU attempted to hold a meeting in Loughborough marketplace, but it was broken up by local youths.
8 January	Christabel Pankhurst, on the death of her brother, failed to attend a WSPU meeting in Northampton Town Hall. She was replaced by Mrs Pethick-Lawrence and others from Clement's Inn in London.
12 January	The WSPU held several lunchtime meetings around Northampton and at factory gates.
12 January	Mrs Emmeline Pankhurst addressed the WSPU General Election meeting in Albert Hall, Nottingham. 'Keep the Liberal Out.'
13 January	The WSPU held a meeting at their temporary HQ in the Committee Rooms at 13 Bridge Street, Northampton.
15 January	Leicester WSPU attempted to hold a meeting in Loughborough's cattle market. Police protected the women.
24 January	The Nottingham WSPU held meeting in Retford. Nellie Crocker and Mrs Douglas-Smith gave a talk on women workers.
26 January	Emmeline Pankhurst attended a meeting in Loughborough. Bertha Clark attended the meeting and helped with the opening of the shop in Baxter Gate, Loughborough.
28 January	Dorothy Pethick confirmed that she was to stay on as Leicester's organiser and opened an office at 17 Highfields Street.
January	General Election. The Liberals are returned.
1 February	Lady Lytton addressed a WSPU meeting in Queen's Hall, Nottingham, and outlined the policy of the hunger strike.
2 February	Nottingham NUWSS collected 8,000 signatures in support of Votes For Women.
2 February	Mrs Emmeline Pankhurst attended WSPU at Circus Hall, Nottingham. She is to oppose Colonel Seeby in the Ilkeston by-election. Dorothy Pethick organised the campaign.
14 February	WSPU declared a truce to allow Conciliation Bill to be read.
25 February	Mrs Emmeline Pankhurst spoke at a WSPU meeting at the Castle Gate Lecture Hall, Nottingham.
28 February	Mrs Emmeline Pankhurst and Charlotte Marsh held meeting in Ilkeston.
1 March	Nellie Crocker held a meeting at Long Eaton, while Dorothy Pethick held a meeting in Heanor marketplace. Emmeline Pankhurst spoke at the Town Hall.
2 March	Colonel Seeby won an election for the Liberals with a majority of 4,000.
5 March	Leicester WSPU held a meeting in Kibworth village hall. Both Mrs Pemberton-Peake and Dorothy Pethick spoke.
8 March	Leicester WSPU opened an official shop in Bowling Green Street.
12 March	Mrs Emmeline Pankhurst attended a meeting in Leicester's Temperance Hall.

19 March	Leicester WSPU held a second meeting at Kibworth village hall.
22 March	The WSPU held a meeting in Circus Street Hall, Nottingham. Mrs Emmeline Pankhurst failed to attend. Isobel Seymour attended instead.
22 April	Leicester WSPU began a campaign in Kibworth and Market Harborough, then open-air meetings at Shepshed, Castle Donington, Syston, Kegworth and Melton.
29 April	Leicester WSPU held an 'At Home' in the Old Town Hall, Belgrave, Leicester.
4 June	Mrs Brailsford, from London, held a meeting a Loughborough's Temperance Hall.
14 June	The Conciliation Bill was introduced into Parliament.
18 June	Both Nottingham, Leicester and Loughborough WSPU took part the procession of 10,000 women from Black Friars Bridge to Albert Hall in London.
11/12 July	No time is further allowed for the Conciliation Bill.
14 July	A joint procession is staged by both the Leicester WSPU and NUWSS.
18 July	A huge WSPU meeting is held in Nottingham's marketplace to demonstrate against the delay in the Franchise Bill.
23 July	Second large London demonstration. Both Leicester & Nottingham WSPU march to Hyde Park.
23 July	Both Leicester WSPU and NUWSS staged a protest in the Temperance Hall at the failing of the Conciliation Bill.
26 July	The Church League for Women's Suffrage attempted to bring all aspects of the suffrage movement to work together in Nottingham. Several WSPU members got involved.
12 August	Leicester WSPU organised a campaign on the Norfolk coast.
18 August	The WSPU sent letter to Nottingham trades council. They ignored the letter.
September	All Autumn 'At Homes' in Leicester were moved to Sunday School Memorial Hall, New Walk, Leicester.
20 September	Charlotte Marsh and Dorothy Pethick spoke at the Town Hall in Nottingham.
29 September	The WSPU held meeting at Morley's Café, Nottingham. Mrs Brailsford expressed concern over the Conciliation Bill.
14 November	Emmeline Pethick-Lawrence attended an 'At Home' in Leicester.
17 November	Emmeline Pethick-Lawrence stood in for Christabel Pankhurst at WSPU meeting in Albert Hall, Nottingham. She attacked Asquith's veto on the Conciliation Bill and informed the meeting of the London demonstration for the following day.
18 November	The Leicester WSPU produced a play entitled *How The Vote was Won* and performed it at the Grand Hotel, Leicester.
18 November	Albert Hall meeting in London. East Midland branches attended.
18 November	Several WSPU members from Nottingham and Leicester were arrested in London on Black Friday. They were Miss Lillian Hickling, Nellie Crocker, Miss Elsie Hall from Nottingham and Miss Katherine Corcoran from Loughborough, and Alice Hawkins, Miss Corrie Swain, Alice Ionides & Dorothy Bowker from Leicester. They were released without charge.
22 November	One-hundred and fifty-six people arrested in London, including Dorothy Pethick, Alice Hawkins, Miss Elizabeth Frisby and Elsa Oswald from Nottingham, and all were sent to prison.
26 November	Mr Albert Hawkins was ejected from Liberal meeting in Bradford. He sued the Liberal Party for £100 damages.
27 November	Loughborough WSPU held a meeting in the Lecture Room in the Town Hall and objected to force-feeding.
3 December	In Leicester, both Alice Pemberton-Peake and Jessie Bennett complained to the *Pioneer* at the treatment of the women in London on Black Friday.
December	The Leicester WSPU opened a special General Election shop at 275 Belgrave Gate during the second General Election.

1911

January	The WSPU resumed their truce.
6 January	Alfred Hawkins of Leicester was honoured in Caxton Hall for his actions in supporting the WSPU.
7 January	In Leicester, both Alice Hawkins and Lizzie Willson elected to Leicester's trades council.
24 January	Dorothy Pethick addressed a meeting of Literary and Debating Society at the Mechanics' Hall in Nottingham. She explained militant tactics.
27 January	Leicester WSPU held a social in Belgrave's Old Town Hall to honour Alfred Hawkins.
4 February	Councillor R.H. Swain asked the Nottingham City Council to support the Conciliation Bill.
11 February	Alice Hawkins appealed to Leicester's trades council to take more action on firms that wage war on trade unionism and anti women in industry.
17 February	Leicester WSPU began a campaign of handing out hand-bills at factory gates.
18 February	Leicester WSPU held a meeting in the Temperance Hall. Christabel Pankhurst spoke.
24 February	Miss Miller began a campaign in Northamptonshire, but with little success.
3 March	Leicester WSPU held a meeting in the Town Hall, Loughborough. Mrs Kineaton Parks, of the Women's Tax Resistance, spoke.
3 March	Leicester WSPU recruited volunteers for the next deputation.
18 March	Leicester WSPU held a meeting at Temperance Hall. Mrs Eates advised them on Census resistance.
23 March	Leicester WSPU attended Albert Hall meeting in London.
2 April	Census Night. The women in Leicester stayed in the shop in Bowling Green Street.
2 April	The Nottingham WSPU spent the night in a private house in Nottingham.
28 April	Miss J. Jerwood, of Little Bowden Rectory, became Market Harborough's WSPU organising secretary.
April	Leicester WSPU asked the local trades council to support the Conciliation Bill.
5 May	Conciliation Bill was again debated.
22 May	A poll held in Nottingham suggested that many Nottingham women did not want the vote.
6 June	Leicester WSPU wrote a letter to the local trades council asking for their support for the Conciliation Bill. They reject the offer by five votes.
17 June	Leicester WSPU attended an Albert Hall meeting and Coronation procession in London.
September	Leicester WSPU began a second campaign in Kettering and Thrapston.
2 September	Alice Hawkins & Lizzie Willson formed the Women's Independent Boot & Shoe Union in Leicester.
October	Miss Miller's Kettering WSPU branch began to falter and she moved to Northampton.
5 October	Alice Hawkins attacked the attitude of Leicester's Boot and Shoe Union towards the WSPU.
11 October	Christabel Pankhurst spoke at a meeting of The Free Church League for Women's Suffrage in the Victoria Hall, Nottingham.
16 October	Leicester WSPU held a meeting in Victoria Galleries, Leicester, to hear Miss Vida Goldstein, from Austria, and Lord Lytton speak.
7 November	By announcing a Manhood Suffrage Bill, Asquith killed the Conciliation Bill.
16 November	Leicester WSPU attended a meeting in the Albert Hall.
18 November	Nottingham WSPU held a meeting in Morley's Café, Nottingham. Mrs Brailsford brought them up to date on the Conciliation Bill.

21 November	Nottingham and Leicester women took part in window-smashing spree in the Strand, London.
28 November	Nottingham and Leicester women attended Bow Street Court. Alice Hawkins, Elizabeth Frisby, Corrie Swain and Lillian Hickling were sent to prison for 21 days.
29 November	Nellie Crocker told the Nottingham WSPU, in Morley's Café, of the events surrounding the arrest of Lillian Hickling.
29 November	100 MP's who once supported the WSPU signed a statement condemning their actions.
11 December	Miss Miller organised a meeting for potential recruits in Northampton.
12 December	Loughborough WSPU held a meeting in the Town Hall. Dorothy Pethick attempted to defend the WSPU's actions in London.
13 December	Leicester WSPU held a meeting in the Corn Exchange. They defend their action in London. They also call on Ramsay MacDonald and the Labour Party to reject the Manhood Bill.
5 December	First meeting of the Northampton WSPU branch held at the County Hall.

1912

1 January	John Burns MP harassed by WSPU in Leicester.
20 January	Nottingham WSPU failed to distract Lord Aldine in Nottingham's Albert Hall. Attempts were weak and sloppy.
27 January	Nottingham WSPU made to look fools when heckling Lincolnshire Farmers' Union.
9 February	Lady Margesson arrived to talk to the new Northampton WSPU in Dr Bentley's house on Sheep Street regarding militancy. Her arguments were rejected by some.
10 February	Christabel Pankhurst arrived in Northampton and addressed a WSPU meeting in the Palace Theatre. She attempted to keep the husbands on board.
10 February	Nottingham WSPU member 'Penelope', wrote a letter to *Nottingham Guardian*. A plea was made for women to come forward and join the movement.
10 February	Mrs Pankhurst attended a WSPU meeting in the Corn Exchange in Leicester to explain a new policy on militancy. Revd Donaldson attended.
21 February	Annie Kenney, keeping up the pressure on the new Northampton branch, gave a talk at the Friendly Society's Hall, Northampton.
1 March	Nottingham Women's organisation formed as an advisory board on the Insurance Act. Nottingham WSPU refuse to get involved.
1 March	Mass window smashing took place in London.
4 March	Further outbreak of window smashing took place.
5 March	Two Northampton WSPU members, Mrs Croft and Mabel Crockett, wrote a letter to the *Northampton Daily Chronicle*, defending militancy and outlining their part in the window smashing in London.
6 March	In London the WSPU HQ was raided and several women were arrested, including Nellie Crocker and Gladys Roberts from Nottingham and Nellie Smithies-Taylor, Dorothy Bowker and Gladys Hazel from Leicester. Christabel Pankhurst escaped to Paris.
6 March	Husband of Northampton WSPU member, Mr Thomas Collier, wrote to the *Northampton Daily Chronicle*, defending the actions of the organisation.
8 March	Mrs Bennett from Leicester was arrested in London for smashing windows.
16 April	Sylvia Pankhurst arrived in East Nottingham to direct a by-election campaign. (Nellie Crocker and Gladys Roberts in prison.) NUWSS declared support for Liberal, but WSPU declined to support either.
26 April	Miss Georgina Brackenbury and Mrs Flora Drummond addressed Leicester WSPU in the Corn Exchange on militancy and the need for Labour men to take up the fight.

1 May	Miss C. Swain from Leicester was arrested in London for breaking windows in New Bond Street. While in prison she was given the organiser's post in Leicester.
10 May	Miss Georgina Brackenbury again addressed the Leicester WSPU in the Corn Exchange. A social was planned to say goodbye to Dorothy Pethick and to welcome Mrs Smithies-Taylor from Holloway Prison, where she had been on hunger strike.
8 June	Nellie Crocker and Gladys Roberts were released from prison. Three days later they were treated to a Welcome Supper in Nottingham.
11 June	Mrs A. Webbe, from London, gave a talk to the Northampton WSPU at the Whyte Melville Hall on the White Slave Trade.
14 June	Dorothy Pethick left the Leicester branch. Miss Swain took temporary control.
18 June	Nottingham WSPU held a meeting in the marketplace. Mrs Drummond and Laura Ainsworth spoke to denounce Colonel Seely.
18 June	Colonel Seely was adopted as Liberal candidate for Ilkeston.
24 June	Nottingham WSPU held a meeting in Ilkeston marketplace.
27 June	Leicester, Market Harborough and Loughborough amalgamated into one Union.
29 June	Laura Ainsworth broke windows in Ilkeston Labour exchange. Mrs Flatman of Nottingham was in charge of the Ilkeston by-election.
July	Leicester WSPU attended Hyde Park demonstration, in London
6 July	Violet Doudney from Leicester was arrested for breaking windows at the residence of the Home Secretary.
17 July	Miss Naylor gave a talk to the Northampton WSPU at the Whyte Melville Hall on the justification of window smashing.
2 August	In line with their non-militant campaign, the Northampton WSPU protest at Colonel Seely's Liberal meeting in the Assembly Hall.
September	WSPU moved their HQ from Clement's Inn to Lincoln's Inn House, Kingsway.
19 October	Lady Isabel Margesson spoke at the Temperance Hall, Leicester. She attempted to justify further acts of militancy.
16 October	Nottingham WSPU held a meeting in Beeston Church Street Schools. Miss Nellie Crocker spoke.
17 October	Mrs Pankhurst announced in the Albert Hall that the Pethick-Lawrences have left. Attended by Leicester and Nottingham branches.
30 October	WSPU reorganised in Leicester and Nottingham. Gladys Hazel, based in Birmingham, took overall control, with Miss Cameron Swain as the local organiser in Leicester and Miss Haley as temporary organiser in Nottingham.
9 November	Pillar box attacks began in London.
12 November	Mrs Sheppard announced that Nellie Crocker and Gladys Roberts have quit the Nottingham WSPU. Miss Haley temporarily takes control under the guidance of Gladice Hazel in Birmingham.
16 November	Leicester WSPU interviewed both Liberal and Labour candidates for local newspaper, the *Pioneer*.
27 November	The Actress Franchise League put on two plays, *The Twelve Pound Lock* and *A Chat With Miss Chicker*, for the benefit of the Northampton WSPU in the Town Hall.
20 November	Pillar boxes attacked in Nottingham as a result of Landsbury's defeat in Bow. Flora Drummond announces working-class deputation.
23 November	The WSPU cause uproar at Liberal Meeting in Nottingham's Albert Hall. Several women are ejected.
4 December	Pillar boxes attacked in Leicester for the first time.
6 December	Leicester's oldest Suffragette, Miss Daring, died at the age of 95. She had been an active suffragist for 50 years.
7 December	Mr Smithies-Taylor from Leicester successfully sued the Liberal Party for assault.

10 December	Nottingham WSPU held a meeting in Friends' School Rooms in Friar Lane. Miss Haley from Birmingham spoke.
11 December	Pillar boxes attacked in Leicester.
13 December	Alice Hawkins and Mrs Newcomer travelled to London to help with the Christmas fair.
16 December	Charlotte Marsh addressed the Northampton WSPU in the Town Hall on the merits on militancy.
30 December	Charlotte Marsh arrived in Nottingham to take control of the branch.

1913

20 January	Mrs Mabel Crockett addressed a Northampton WSPU meeting in the Town Hall.
23 January	Alice Hawkins from Leicester attended a working-class deputation to Lloyd George with Mrs Drummond.
25 January	Northampton WSPU member Mary Crockett wrote letter to *Northampton Mercury* demanding votes for working women.
28 January	Militant demonstration at the House of Commons by the working-women's deputation.
22 January	Charles Hicking wrote a letter to the *Nottingham Daily Express* supporting militancy and accuses Hobhouse of incitement.
28 January	Mrs Pankhurst declared a guerrilla war.
1 February	15 pillar boxes are attacked in Nottingham.
7 February.	Pillar boxes attacked in Nottingham.
19 February	Police foil attack on links at Bulwell Golf Club.
19 February	Annie Kenney addressed two WSPU meetings in Northampton.
19 February	Attempted destruction of letters in Northampton box.
20 February	Pillar boxes are attacked in Mansfield.
21 February	Golf courses attacked across the country. Leicester Golf Club attacked.
24 February	Pillar boxes attacked with phosphorus in Beeston.
25 February	Pillar boxes attacked in Mansfield.
25 February	WSPU interrupted Sir James Yoxall meeting in Stanley Street School, Nottingham. six or seven women forcibly ejected.
27 February	30 Pillar boxes attacked in Nottingham.
28 February	*Nottingham Daily Express* interviewed Charlotte Marsh regarding acts of militancy.
10 March	The Nottingham WSPU attacked a stretch of railway 'On The Forest'.
11 March	Annie Kenney's WSPU meeting in Circus Street Hall, Nottingham, is attacked by men.
13 March	Nottingham Watch Committee received a claim for damages from Circus Street Hall. The claim was later (May 1913) rejected and the Chief Constable responded that all halls must take responsibility for all damages.
25 March	The Cat and Mouse Act is passed.
3 April	Mrs Pankhurst was sent to prison for three years.
9 April	Mrs Suthern's Haystack on the Woolerton Road is destroyed by fire, causing £100 damage.
12 April	*Pioneer* interviewed Miss West in the WSPU shop in Bowling Green Street, Leicester.
15 April.	Charles Rothera wrote a letter in the *Nottingham Daily Express* supporting militancy.
17 April	Pillar boxes are attacked in Nottingham.
25 April	In Northampton, Miss Elsie Miller resigned as organiser. Mrs Mabel Crockett takes over the position. Mrs Collier is made Treasurer.
26 April	WSPU attempted to disrupt Mr Acland MP's meeting in Nottingham's Albert Hall. He was Under Secretary of Foreign Affairs.
28 April	32 Telephone wires are cut in Leicester.

2 May	The Nottingham WSPU gave a lecture on social morality and women's franchise in a private house. No public hall was available.
13 May	Nottingham Boat Club is destroyed by fire.
17 May	Nottingham WSPU withdrew all financial support from church causes.
23 May	Miss Tyson from London attempted to hold a meeting in Leicester's marketplace. The meeting was broken up by a hostile crowd. Alice Hawkins and her daughter were attacked.
25 May	Pillar boxes were attacked in Leicester. Alice Hawkins is arrested and imprisoned.
30 May	A WSPU meeting broken up in Leicester marketplace.
30 May	The Leicester WSPU shop in Bowling Green Street had its windows smashed.
31 May	A hoax suffragette bomb is found in Nottingham.
3 June	Leicester Watch Committee tried to ban WSPU meetings in public places.
6 June	15,000 people assembled in Leicester marketplace looking for the WSPU. Many clash with police and innocent women were attacked.
9 June	Telephone wires are cut in Nottingham. Response to Emily Wilde-Davison's death.
10 June	Despite recent troubles, Leicester WSPU continued to hold meetings in the marketplace.
15 June	Crawshay-Williams, Liberal MP for Leicester, resigned, creating a by-election. A concerted campaign was undertaken by the WSPU.
20 June	The Leicester WSPU appealed to the working class not to vote Liberal.
23 June	The Leicester WSPU organised a massive grand parade through the town.
23 June	The Leicester WSPU continued meetings in the marketplace.
25 June	Miss Naylor addressed the WSPU meeting in Temperance Hall, Leicester.
30 June	Charles Rothera wrote a letter to the *Nottingham Guardian* attacking the Cat and Mouse Act.
5 July	Charles Rothera wrote a letter to the *Nottingham Daily Express* attacking the Cat and Mouse Act.
7 July	Nottingham WSPU held a rowdy meeting in the marketplace. Charlotte Marsh spoke from the back of a dray.
17 July	Nottingham trades council rejected the WSPU's request to condemn the Cat and Mouse Act.
29 July	The WSPU held a meeting in Nottingham's marketplace from four wagonettes around the square. Four London speakers attended.
30 July	Northampton ILP held a meeting in the marketplace to protest against the Cat and Mouse Act. Local WSPU members attended but did not speak.
3 August	Protest chanting interrupted the Litany in St Paul's. Protest chanting begins.
9 August	The WSPU attempted to set fire to Central School in Forest Gate in Sutton in Ashfield.
9 August	The Nottingham WSPU attempted to disrupt Lloyd George's meeting to the miners in Sutton in Ashfield on his Insurance Act.
15 August	The Northampton WSPU held a meeting against the Cat and Mouse Act in the marketplace. The meeting was broken up by local youths.
20 August	Northampton trades council censure local police for their inaction at WSPU meeting.
22 August	Northampton trades council held a public meeting in the marketplace to demonstrate public support for the WSPU and to condemn the Cat and Mouse Act.
1 October	The WSPU attended an anti-suffrage meeting in Shaftsbury Hall.
10 October	Leicester WSPU heckled Ramsay MacDonald. The Labour Party offered Miss Grew the chance to address the meeting at the end. She accepted.
13 October	Charlotte Marsh wrote a letter to the *Nottingham Daily Express* condemning the Cat and Mouse Act.

13 October	WSPU supporter George Meadows wrote two letters to the *Nottingham Guardian*. He suggested he was part of the movement.
19 October	Leicester WSPU attempted to set fire to Red House mansion, Loughborough.
21 October	The WSPU held a meeting in Nottingham marketplace. Charlotte Marsh attempted to speak.
23 October	The WSPU threatened to attack ballot papers in Nottingham's local election.
10 November	Nottingham member Penelope wrote a letter to the *Nottingham Guardian* supporting militant actions.
10 November	Nottingham WSPU disrupted Richard Granger's Liberal meeting in the Castle Gate Lecture Hall. Several women were ejected.
12 November	The WSPU organised a protest meeting in the Corn Exchange with eminent citizens of Nottingham to condemn the Cat and Mouse Act.
16 November	The WSPU interrupted a service at St Mary's Church, Nottingham.
17 November	The WSPU interrupted Sir Yoxall MP's meeting in Forest Road Council School, Nottingham. Several women were ejected.
21 November	Pink liquid was poured in a pillar box in Ilkeston after Charlotte Marsh attended the WSPU in the town.
23 November	Charlotte Marsh interrupted Dr John Massie's Liberal meeting in Nottingham. She was removed by force.
30 November	Charlotte Marsh wrote to Asquith to see if he would meet the Nottingham WSPU when he came to Nottingham. M. Bonar Carter wrote back declining the offer.
30 November	The WSPU opened offices at 46 Bridlesmith Gate. This was Charles Rothera's Nottingham office.
30 November	Pillar boxes were attacked in 10 different Nottingham districts.
1 December	The WSPU disrupted a service at St Andrew's Church, Nottingham.
5 December	Gladys Hazel spoke at a WSPU meeting in Temperance Hall, Leicester.
6 December	The Nottingham WSPU threw leaflets from several local theatre balconies in a publicity stunt.
10 December	The WSPU held a meeting in Friends' Schoolrooms, Friar Lane. Miss Haley spoke.
10 December	Charlotte Marsh announced a campaign to recruit working women.
15 December	The Nottingham WSPU chant Litany at All Saints' Church, Nottingham.
18 December	Flora Drummond stood in for Mrs Pankhurst at a WSPU meeting in Nottingham Corn Exchange.
20 December	Telephone wires were cut in Nottingham.
22 December	The Nottingham WSPU again chant a Litany at All Saints' Church, Nottingham.

1914

1 January	Miss Elizabeth Grew was appointed as Organising Secretary to the Leicester branch.
6 February	Margaret West took over Leicester branch from Miss Grew.
19 February	Haystack fire at Bullwell. £100 worth of damage.
28 February	Mrs Sheppard addressed the Conservative Club in Castle Ward, Nottingham.
25 February	Ramsay MacDonald was heckled by the WSPU in the De Montfort Hall, Leicester.
11 March	Dutch Barn fire at Bulcote, Nottingham. £2,000 damage.
20 March	Ramsay MacDonald was heckled by Leicester WSPU in De Montfort Hall
31 March	Miss Naylor addressed a WSPU meeting in Victoria Galleries, Leicester.
4 April	The Leicester branch attended a rally in Hyde Park, London.
23 April	Kitty Marion was released from prison after being force-fed over 232 times. She went to help Leicester branch organise its arson campaign.
30 April	Dorothy Pethick left for America with Margaret Hodge.
1 May	Northampton WSPU held a meeting in the Town Hall where Miss Naylor spoke.
15 May	St Peter's Church was attacked by Northampton WSPU. They only left WSPU leaflets.

22 May	Northampton WSPU asked for, and received, the support of their local trades council.
23 May	Pillar boxes in Leicester were attacked with black fluid.
23 May	Colwick Park racecourse. Horseboxes set ablaze.
25 May	Shop windows were attacked in Market Street, Leicester.
29 May	A Northampton member, Miss Margaret Capell, left the branch to get married and emigrate to Uganda.
22 May	The Leicester WSPU attempted to burn down Stoughton Hall.
1 June	The Leicester WSPU attempted to burn down Neville Holt mansion house near Market Harborough.
8 June	All Saints' Church in Breadsall was gutted by fire.
11 June	Miss McCauley spoke at the WSPU meeting in Friends' Schoolrooms, Friar Lane.
12 June	94 branches of the Labour Party banned the WSPU from their platforms.
15 June	The WSPU interrupted a service in St Andrew's Church, Nottingham.
15 June	Windows were smashed for the second time in a week at the WSPU shop in Derby Road.
24 June	Pillar boxes were attacked to mark a Royal visit in Nottingham.
25 June	Irene Casey was arrested on the King's Visit to Nottingham.
29 June	The WSPU interrupted a service in St Mary's Church, Nottingham.
3 July	Irene Casey appeared in court.
17 July	Ellen Sheriff, Elizabeth Frisby and Kitty Marion successfully burnt down Blaby Railway station in Leicester, causing £500 worth of damage.
1 August	Dr Helena Jones spoke at a WSPU meeting in Friends' Schoolrooms, Friar Lane, Nottingham.
4 August	War was declared with Germany.
10 August	Mrs Pankhurst suspended militancy.

WSPU MEMBERSHIP FOR LEICESTER 1907–14.

This is, by no means, a definitive list of all members who participated in the WSPU in Leicester. However, it is a list of all the members who have come to light through the variety of sources consulted. Yet I am sure there were many who more [sic] supported the movement and remained unknown.

List of Members

Kitty Marion	Actress came to Leicester from London.
Alice Hawkins	18 Mantel Road, Leicester.
Miss Wells	Travelled to London, February 1907.
Miss Knight	Travelled to London, February 1907.
Mrs Catlin	Wife of ILP Member. Travelled to London, February 1907.
Elizabeth Grew	
Mrs Lowe	Married to Local Counsellor, W.H. Lowe, 18 Harrow Road, Leicester.
Mrs Barnes	46 Harrow Road, Leicester.
Mrs Wills	House keeper, travelled to London in February 1907.
Miss Margaret West	Organiser, July 1914.
Eva Lines	School Teacher
Jane Lavina Wyatt	School Teacher, taught at Harrison Road School.
Ada Billington	School Teacher
Miss Gladys Hazel	Organiser, November 1912 (based in Birmingham).
Miss Evelyn Close	
Miss A.S. (Bertha) Clark	
Miss Evelyn Carryer	Rough Close, St Johns Road, Poor Law Guardian.
Dorothy Pethick	Came to Leicester in January 1910 as organiser, 11 Severn Street.
Isobel Logan	The Grange East Langton, Market Harborough, daughter of Liberal MP.
Mrs Johnson	Went London in February 1907.
Ellen Sheriff	One of three who attacked Blaby Railway Station.
Dorothy Bowker	Companion to Dorothy Pethick.
Mrs F.W. Bennett	Known as Jesse Bennett, 104 Regents Road.
Alice Pemberton-Peake	21 Oxford Street, wife of Dr Pemberton-Peake.
Laura Ainsworth	Came to Leicester from hunger strike in Winston Green as organiser, October 1909.
Mr & Mrs Smithies-Taylor	2 Newarke Street.

SOME IMPRESSIONS OF PRISON LIFE – HM PRISON HOLLOWAY
In Alice's own words

Being sentenced to 14 days at Westminster for asking for the rights of women. We were held at Westminster Police Court until after 3 o'clock. We were then brought in a Black Maria and arrived about 4 o'clock. I felt rather sorry for the female officers when about 60 were handed to them at once. It made a great deal of work for them. They had to place us in the cells 6 to 8 together so that we passed the time fairly well until they could get the cells ready for us, which was not until 10 o'clock at night. Some were even later than that when we arrived in our separate cells we were told to get our beds ready. This consisted of a mattress and pillows, a pair of rough blankets and a counterpane, but as you may imagine, there was not much sleep for me in such a bed.

We had to get up at 6 o'clock had breakfast about 7 and clean all up in our cells and be ready for chapel by 8 o'clock, which lasts until about 9.15. Then we had a visit from the doctor if needed and the Governor if you want to ask for anything. About 10 o'clock you go out for exercise which consists of walking around a few paths of gravel for about a hour after which we do as we like in our cells. Either we sew or write until dinner time.

The afternoon is lonely as we see no one till tea time between 4 and 5, unless a warder lets us out to empty any dirty water we may have. After tea we are locked in again until morning and so on day after day, excepting Sunday when we go to Church twice. I may say we are allowed a book twice a week and after the first Sunday we had a newspaper so that we were not altogether without news from the outer world.

Now this is the daily routine for the 1st class prisoners. I don't think the others are allowed anything nearly as well as this. As for food, it is just enough to keep a person alive providing they can eat it. Every morning we got a pint of tea and a small loaf of brown bread. Dinner is slightly better as there is a change each day. One day we had haricot beans and potatoes, another day pressed meat and potatoes and another suet pudding and potatoes with brown bread and so on through the 14 days. Tea time we get, a pint of cocoa and a loaf of brown bread.

But oh the long, long nights from 8 o'clock when the electric light is put out until 6 in the morning when it's turned on again. Lying on a hard mattress until every bone in your body aches and you are only too pleased to see the light again so that you may get on your feet again.

Some of the faces I saw were rather interesting. One in particular, that I saw in church set me thinking, 'what ever could have brought her to prison?' She was a girl not more than 16 with, oh, such a sweet face and pathetic eyes. I could not keep my eyes off her every time we went to church. But I should think there were quite 500 women and girls going to church every Sunday. Some with such lovely faces. It was almost impossible to think they could have committed any crime. Some looked very down hearted, but many were quite cheerful.

When we were out for exercise, I saw women put to some fearfully heavy work, such as stoking and pushing trucks about loaded with very heavy looking material and carrying heavy loads of water and provisions. And I also saw women pulling garden rollers along, in fact, it seemed, as far as I could find out, that women do all the work for the gardens of the prison specified by them.

One day, whilst at exercise, I saw a number of women with babies in their arms, and, on asking the warders about them, she informed me that they were allowed to have their babies under 12 months, and said they were well looked after. But, oh the thought that a young life just born into the world should have to spend its first months of life in prison. It was one more injustice added to our cry for the right to stop some of these horrible things being allowed. For I am quite convinced that a great alteration could be made to our prison lives.

The regulations are very strict, we are not allowed to speak to each other, neither at church or exercise. But of course, we manage to have a word now and again. The prison itself is beautifully clean, very little wood is used in its construction, so there is not much fear of fire.

Our cells are lit by electricity and a bell is fitted in each cell, but you might ring it 20 times a day and not get it answered, unless it happens that the matron, governor or Chaplin were in the corridor. Many's the time my heart as ached for the poor women that are in for hard labour, for it is one long grind from early morning until late at night. I have just had a visit from the Chaplin wishing me God's speed and good-bye.

Alice Hawkins, February 1907.

equity
shoes

Equity Shoes Ltd, which was established in 1886, is where Alice Hawkins worked as a machinist during the late 1800s and early 1900s.

At that stage of the Victorian era it was a period of change, covering social, political and economic life. It is believed that Alice was drawn to the work ethic that Equity was founded upon: equality of opportunity and rewards for everyone regardless of sex or class.

Equity Shoes Ltd was formed by a group of disillusioned employees of a large manufacturer in the city. They decided that they would form a 'true productive establishment', and a meeting was held in St Margaret's Coffee House on Friday 16 September 1885. Around 60 people were present, and the name 'The Leicester Co-operative Boot and Shoe Manufacturing Society' was adopted. (This was changed to Equity Shoes Ltd in the early 1900s.)

A subscription list was opened, a membership list was made out and for the next few months they met each week, making plans for the new venture. Money was raised in the form of a subscription, where they paid sixpence or a shilling each week, and by September 1886 the first balance sheet showed £96 1s 11d cash in the bank.

The first premises were leased – three rooms in Friar's Causeway – and 21 people commenced work there in the spring of 1887.

By midsummer 1889 the society had grown so much that larger premises had to be leased in Bede Street for £180.00 per annum. Towards the end of the five-year lease, a decision was made to build a factory in Western Road. The new premises were occupied in January 1895 and this building remains the manufacturing premises for Equity Shoes Ltd today, although several extensions for further production, offices and warehousing have been added over the years.

Equity currently employs 150 people and manufactures 6,000 pairs per week, making Equity one of the largest shoe factories in the country. This is perhaps a sad reflection on the footwear industry, when, not too many years ago, there were upwards of 50 shoe manufacturers in Leicestershire alone.

We believe that the business ethics and principles of our founders are still maintained today, and this is a factor in our being able to continue to produce quality footwear in these difficult times.

This book pays tribute to Alice Hawkins and her colleagues for their determination and principles, for which they suffered personal hardship. Their cause remains one of the most potent achievements of 20th-century political and social history.

Equity Shoes is proud to have played a small part in her story.

J.A. Greaves
President, Equity Shoes Ltd, October 2006

TUC

'The path you take up the mountain as a successful woman was uncovered by the generations of women who went before you; and your mountain peak is simply a foothold for the generations who will follow.'

Baroness Crawley, Former Chair, Women's National Commission

To refer to Alice Hawkins as an organiser seems somewhat inadequate. The word is simply not large enough to fully explain the sheer energy, political commitment and bravery of Alice. The activities of Alice in founding and organising the suffragette movement in Leicester would be reason enough to celebrate her amazing yet, sadly, far too unheralded contribution to equality, but so is her contribution to the trade union movement.

Working men and women owe a major debt of gratitude to the work that Alice did to help to improve terms and conditions in the boot and shoe factories of the region. Consequently, the trade union movement owes much to Alice for helping to build strong trade unionism in the area. Trade unionism is about enabling working people to organise and stand up for their rights at work and beyond. Alice Hawkins made a major contribution to that goal.

An understanding of this period in history, which I am sure you will get from this book, will leave you staggered at the difficulties working people faced and those who worked hard to help them. Few people faced and overcame these difficulties better than Alice Hawkins. It has never been easy to stand up against the tide and to try to overturn public opinion or so-called received wisdoms. To stand up and say things that some people don't want to hear – to speak truth to power – takes a special kind of bravery that far too often is only attributed to men. This nails that myth once again – let us hope that it does so once and for all.

The point about history is not to live in it but to learn from it and to be inspired to continue the legacy that has been passed down to us. The fight for the vote for women was just part of the fight for equality. We still today have not secured the equality for women to get paid the same as men for doing the same work. We still have far too many jobs considered to be women's jobs and therefore attracting lower pay. Women still face widespread discrimination and harassment in the workplace. All of these continuing fights owe their lineage to the brave women, such as Alice Hawkins, who fought for the right for women to vote. To truly celebrate their legacy we need to draw strength from this book to help us in the continuing struggle for equality for women.

Roger McKenzie
Regional Secretary Midlands Trades Union Congress

Alice Hawkins place of burial

Until recently, the whereabouts of Alice's burial was unknown. At a reunion of the family, great-grandson Jim Beadman presented this cemetery grant document which identifies her burial at the Welford Road Cemetery. The family have plans to locate the plot and erect a memorial as part of the 2007 celebrations. Watch this space.

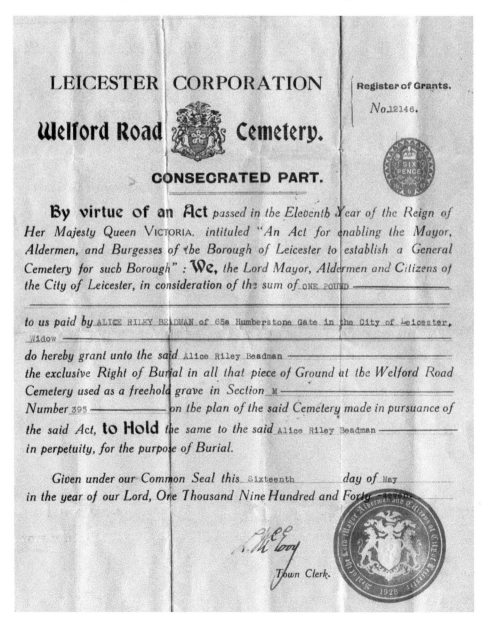

Search for Suffragette descendents

Standing (L to R): Jim Beadman, Barbara Salmon, Pat Maloney, Rt Hon Patricia Hewitt, Sue Anderson, Peter Barratt. Seated: Madge Kemp.
All those standing except for Patricia are great-grandchildren of Alice. Madge is one of three remaining grandchildren. Patricia is holding the original Votes for Women banner that Alice wore, and Madge is holding her medal.

Alice Hawkins's family, her three remaining grandchildren, many great-grandchildren and great-great-grandchildren celebrate her life and legacy. On November 28 the Rt Hon Patricia Hewitt hosted Madge Kemp and several of Alice's descendants in a little celebration of her life at the House of Commons.

The family and the LeicestHERday Trust are not only looking for more descendents of Alice and Alfred Hawkins, but also for relatives of other Midlands suffragettes who can join us in the celebration of the centenary, 1907 to 2007, a Century of Change and Challenge.

If you are one of these people or know of someone who can follow this trail, please call us at LeicestHERday Trust on 0116 257 5615 or e-mail us at leicestherday@blleics.co.uk.

Check the progress of this search on www.leicestherday.org.uk

LeicestHERday

'I am a woman, hear me roar / In numbers too big to ignore, /
And I know too much / To go back and pretend.'
Helen Reddy, American Singer/Composer

When the great-grandson of Alice Hawkins contacted us to inform us of the centenary opportunity that existed in 2007, our members were excited about the prospects of celebrating the life of a woman who had given 'all' to a single-minded goal in obtaining votes for women.

That was 1907 and we obtained the right to vote in 1928.

In 2007 the LeicestHERday Trust is delighted to celebrate her centenary by setting the theme for our 2007 conference: Alice Hawkins, her legacy, 1907 to 2007.

We have been given a great opportunity by Alice's family to further our work in her name as Honorary Patron of the LeicestHERday Trust.

This means not only a book about her struggle, but also creating work in her name to continue our 'her'story, to share her and our stories with the community at large. We need to inform and motivate our young people and involve them in the celebration.

We need to tell Alice's story to all sections of society that have similar experiences of oppression who can understand the frustration of overcoming barriers to their dreams and goals.

Alice and her family have given us an amazing opportunity and challenge.

LeicestHERday Trust accepts this challenge to celebrate achievement as well as engage and empower other women who, like Alice, are passionate about their work, homes and communities and want the right to aspire, dream and achieve.

Maureen

Maureen Milgram Forrest,
Founding Chair on behalf of
The LeicestHERday Trust

LeicestHERday's 2006 launch.

ND - #0292 - 270225 - C0 - 234/156/12 - PB - 9781780911274 - Gloss Lamination